A Man Called
Glader
The Emigrants

About people like Vilhelm Moberg's emigrants
Kristina and Karl Oskar

A Man Called Glader

The Emigrants

by Bodil Stefansson

Excerpts from *En man som hetade Glader*

Translated from the original Swedish by
Bodil Stefansson
and
John Linn

About people like Vilhelm Moberg's emigrants
Kristina and Karl Oskar

ISBN: 978-1-7347379-2-9

printing: 1st

layout and graphics design: John Linn
cover photo: Ingvar Malmberg

The cover is a photo of the Karl Oskar and Kristina monument in downtown Lindstrom, Minnesota. The statue is a replica of the original sculpted by Axel Olsson, which is located in Karlshamn, Blekinge, Sweden. Karlshamn is the port city from which many early Småland emigrants started their trans-Atlantic voyage to America. Karl Oskar looks optimistically forward to the new land while Kristina hesitantly looks back at her last glimpse of Sweden.

Seminal Books
Richardson TX

A visit to Glader Cemetery

Elin Glader's Grave. Photo: Courtesy Robert B. Porter.

In 1948, Vilhelm Moberg lived in Chisago County Minnesota for several hot summer weeks gathering material for his novel about emigration from Sweden. At the old Indian lake Ki Chi Saga he found the place where Karl Oskar and Kristina would settle and live. Now the author was searching for somewhere to bury them.

Editor Ted Norelius of the Chisago County Press guided Moberg to the oldest Swedish cemetery in Minnesota. In front of them, the country rose to a gentle hill. Its north side had been carved out by wind and water and descended abruptly into Lake Ki Chi Saga. At last they located Glader Cemetery.

Old and weathered tombstones peeked out at them from above the tall grass and poison ivey. Some inscriptions were impossible to read because the sandstone had worn smooth over time. The oldest tomb was that of Elin Glader from Ljuder. She had been buried in 1855 next to the lake and close to her home—but far from the nearest church.

Vilhelm Moberg pushed aside the grass from one tombstone after an other, all the while reading the inscriptions. The language was archaic but the names were familiar. After exploring the cemetery, he proclaimed: "This is where I'm going to bury Karl Oskar and Kristina!"

Table of Contents

List of Illustrations

Preface to the English edition
A Man Named Glader

Between 1850–1930 more than a million Swedes emigrated to North America. The author Vilhelm Moberg gave their history eternal life. His fictional Karl Oskar and Kristina left the poor province of Småland to create a better life at Ki Chi Saga (Chisago Lake) in Minnesota.

En man som hetade Glader is a historical chronicle about the first Smålanders who undertook the same journey. By unraveling the destiny of several emigrants like Moberg's leading characters, we get to know the real-life Karl Oskars and Kristinas. The focal point of these stories is the sociable and strong Anders Peter Glader, who remained an obstinate optimist though he endured many hardships in life.

I: Swedish Roots
By following Glader and his ancestors—with a special emphasis on the women—life in Sweden 1750–1850 is revealed. The story starts with the small familiar matters of everyday life. It also is vital to place these people in a historical context. Over time a growing population reduced available land and poverty spread, while strict laws of state and church stifled social improvement. When hard work and ambitions did not guarantee survival, the most resolute decided to change their destiny by emigrating to North America.

II: The Emigrants
These Swedes packed food and other necessities in travel chests and sold all other properties. They left their home and family, going on a one-way journey with no expectation of ever returning. After the dangerous Atlantic voyage, the immigrants travelled by overcrowded trains and boats over lakes, plains and rivers to Chisago Lake. Using the skills and strengths from the old country to survive on the frontier, the immigrants started turning the wild woods into their new homes.

Life was hard but the settlers now were their own masters. The pioneer families around Chisago Lake strove to establish the society they desired. Most kept their old ways, even after becoming Americans.

III - A Good Land

At the end of the 1850s Minnesota Native Americans no longer could survive living their traditional way. Both the Ojibwe and their enemies, the Dakotas, were confined to reservations. At times, they visited their old hunting grounds and there our Swedish settlers occasionally would meet them.

Around Chisago Lake, the most attractive land was already claimed and some of the immigrants were fed up with creating fertile fields from virgin forests. When the "Swedish Indian" Jacob Fahlström spoke about the verdunt Kandiyohi Prairie he planted a seed among the Smålanders. In 1857 the county was surveyed and settlers were given the right to claim land. Once more, the most daring went west to the new frontier. It took courageous and tough men and women to cope with pioneer life, both at Chisago Lake and in Kandiyohi county. Glader's youngest sister Cathrina and her family were among the first to go west. Four years later all settlers in Kandiyohi County had to flee for their lives in the beginning of the devastating Dakota War.

When the Civil War started, Glader's sons and his future son-in-laws volunteered to fight for their new homeland. They participated in battles down south and served in Minnesota during the Dakota war and its aftermath.

Even before the 2017 release of the "Glader book" in Sweden, Americans requested an English translation. We decided to start with the chapters about Smålanders who made a dramatic and life-changing decision to leave their homes and emigrate to the wilds of North America.

May we introduce—*The Emigrants!*

Bodil Stefansson and John Linn
Dec 22nd 2020

From humble beginnings…

A wealthy immigrant farmer's two-story home.
Photo: Courtesy Duane Lunemann.

Most early pioneers came to America impoverished, but still hopeful. They wanted to become wealthy farmers and own vast acres of land. And most of all, they wanted to have a house their neighbors recognized as the residence of a person of prominence and success.

But success did not come instantly or easily for Moberg's protagonists, nor for the real-life Swedish immigrants either. This painting was created by an unknown artist, possibly in the late 1880s. It reflected 35 years of investment—tilling the ground and toiling in the woods—since Carl Linn's arrival in America. Carl's granddaughter described the results of her grandfather's aspirations: "He could look out the window, look around, and he owned as far as he could see! · · · Carl Linn had come a long way! He had achieved things, things that people today can hardly imagine."

This was not Carl's first house. The very first house he built was rumored to be the small log-cabin out-building in the left foreground of the painting.

1

About a poor Östgötlander who came to be a settler at Ki Chi Saga Lake thanks to the world-famous soprano Jenny Lind

Rescue arrived at the last moment for the Östgötlander Anders Svensson. He and his family were filled with anticipation as they stood on the deck of the sailing ship Skogman as it arrived in New Orleans in the autumn of 1850. Anders was 33 years old and his wife Katarina (Cajsa) Petersdotter was a year his senior. In August, they left their home in Kättilstad parish with three children: Gustav seven years old, Johanna age three and John age two. They first traveled to Motala where their journey continued on the Göta Canal to Gothenburg. After eight weeks of sailing the family finally approached the country of their dreams—but soon met with shocking reality.

From New Orleans near the Gulf of Mexico one could travel into the heart of America on the mighty Mississippi River. Anders and Cajsa had planned to settle near Chicago but their best plans were thwarted. Like many other Swedish immigrants they were naturally trusting and accepting. New Orleans was a frightening place with its multitude of people and languages and it felt like a godsend when a man suddenly appeared speaking in Swedish. He knew the city well and offered his help, but it didn't take long before the stranger stole the wallet with all the family's life savings. Anders bought tickets north as far as the money he had in his pocket would go, but they became stranded in St. Louis—without money, in an unknown country, where people spoke a foreign language. During the winter of 1850–51 Anders Svensson supported his family by loading and unloading steamers. On the journey across the Atlantic Cajsa had become pregnant and now in very primitive conditions gave birth to a daughter. With the spring came the rain and in March the rain never stopped. The streets of St. Louis turned into a sea of mud. At the same time the city suffered a cholera epidemic and Anders and Cajsa's children fell ill. Both the elder son Gustav and the infant daughter died and there was no money to bury them. Their situation was desperate.

At that time, the world-famous Swedish singer Jenny Lind was making a successful tour in America. When her ship arrived in New York in 1850 she was welcomed by more than 30,000 cheering Americans, though no one yet had even heard her sing. In Europe she was already an established star who performed for Queen Victoria in England and became known for attracting huge masses of people. This got the American entertainment organizer and publicity genius P. T. Barnum to invest heavily in marketing "the Swedish nightingale" with her fantastic voice and outstanding charisma. The singer enthralled her audience everywhere and all of America caught Jenny Lind fever. The first ticket sold was auctioned off for $225. Her excellent reputation was further strengthened by the charity work she did in the cities she visited. In New Orleans, Baroness Pontalba[1] made a luxury apartment available to Jenny Lind for free. Every evening Jenny appeared on the balcony facing Jackson Square where thrilled crowds of Americans tossed flowers up to her and applauded. The concerts were well attended and the celebrated singer earned a lot of money, even though most of the proceeds went to the promoter Barnum.

When the "nightingale from Sweden" left the city the Baroness auctioned off all the furniture from the Jenny Lind suite. Everything was sold to the highest bidder, even the chamber pot. Whatever the famous soprano touched brought a high price and the auction generated a significant profit for the New Orleans' smartest businesswoman. In mid March Barnum's great American tour reached St. Louis and Pastor Gustav Unonius took the opportunity to visit Jenny Lind to solicit another contribution for his Swedish congregation in Chicago.

Gustav Unonius arrived in America in 1841 with his wife, housekeeper and three of his friends. For the blue-eyed student from Uppsala, the hardship at his new home in the Wisconsin forests had become an ordeal. Despite this, he wrote encouraging articles to Swedish newspapers and attracted his countrymen to follow in his footsteps. When Fredrika Bremer[2] made her famous trip to America in 1849–51, she visited Unonius at Pine Lake. After a few years the Swedish academician, tired of hard life in the wilderness, educated himself to become a Presbyterian minister.

Anders Svensson's family endured much grief in St. Louis, but finally the Östgötlander made a connection with Jenny Lind. The story of their dire straits touched the singer. She was ready to donate $75 to the children's funeral and the family's interrupted journey if Anders Svensson promised to settle in Minnesota. Gustav Unonius advised the Östgötlander to settle down at the beautiful lake Ki Chi Saga where his friend Eric Norberg intended to create a new Swedish settlement. A survey had already been completed and the land was now open to homesteading.

At the lake the Ojibwe Indians called Ki Chi Saga (large and beautiful water) Norberg found the perfect place for Swedish settlers. The v-shaped lake consisted of two lobed arms surrounded by a dense forest. Around it grew maple, ash, basswood, oak, elm, cedar and walnut trees. Many different kinds of berries grew in abundance. Here and there the forest opened into meadows where the soil was good. On the beach of today's Center City, Erik Norberg first stayed in a dugout hut covered with elm bark. Later he settled in a small log cabin about ½ mile outside Taylors Falls. From this cabin he wrote letters to Swedish immigrants in America to attract them to the area's many assets. A map was attached to each letter and the recipients were asked to copy everything and circulate it to others.

> Eric Ulric Norberg was a former sheriff [*länsman*] in Västergötland. After financial irregularities were discovered in 1842 he and his sister had to escape to North America. They spent the first Christmas with Gustav Unonius and his wife at Pine Lake, Wisconsin. Four years later, Norberg joined the Janssonites at Bishop Hill, Illinois, where he married and became quite influential. The sect's leader Erick Jansson became increasingly dictatorial, which aggravated the congregation. He was shot and killed in 1850. When Eric Norberg subsequently failed to gain greater power in Bishop Hill, he instead moved to Minnesota territory to start a new Swedish settlement.

Per "Joris Pelle" Andersson was a wealthy and literate farmer from Hassela parish in Hälsingland. He became the leader of a group of emigrants arriving to New York in November 1850. Their journey continued toward Bishop Hill, Illinois, but Joris Pelle did not want to join the Jansonites. His ancestors were among the Finnish immigrants who settled in the Hälsingland forest. Per thrived in wide forests with good hunting and fishing. For him it was unthinkable to settle on the open prairies of Illinois and he found farming uninteresting. Then he received a letter from Eric Norberg describing a beautiful lake with abundant fish and surrounded by virgin fertile land and mighty forests full of game. This was exactly what Joris Pelle longed for.

With spring approaching, three families along with some bachelors set out for Lake Ki Chi Saga, located near Taylors Falls in the Minnesota territory. In early April 1851 the northern part of the Mississippi River was covered with ice. The steamboat The Yankee had been docked for the winter but now was ready for the season's first trip to Minnesota. On April 15, the canal south of St. Paul through Lake was opened. The Yankee embarked from Galena, Illinois. On board were Östgötlander Anders Svensson and his wife and children. The family had escaped misery and cholera in St. Louis and they were on the way to becoming settlers in Minnesota. Anders met Joris Pelle's party in Galena and joined them for the journey to Ki Chi Saga.

A few days after the Swedes arrived at St. Paul, the city's residents saw a newspaper article describing four families arriving on The Yankee and then continuing on to join Mr. Norberg at Big Lake. The article mentioned that Swedes were good farmers, had good moral values and were diligent and frugal. It said people like these would contribute to building Minnesota. [Por12]

The immigrants continued their journey up the St. Croix River to the town of Stillwater which lay in a beautiful setting at the northern point where the sailors of the great Mississippi River could dock. The St. Croix River upstream was narrow, fast flowing, mostly shallow and could only be traversed by smaller steamboats. However, the ice situation was unknown and the skipper could not provide any guarantees as to how far up the river he could sail.

The Swedes decided to stay in Stillwater while three of the men traveled by road to Taylors Falls. Anders Svensson from Östergötland, Per Wicklund from Medelpad and Joris Pelle's farmhand Daniel Rättig from Hälsingland departed on the well-trodden path to Taylors Falls. There they quickly found Norberg who showed them to Ki Chi Saga. After spending the night in the forest the men surveyed the area and were satisfied with the location. Early the next morning they returned to Stillwater 30 miles away.

The Swedes wanted to get to Ki Chi Saga and so they hired a man for five dollars a day to help with transportation of people and goods. On a shallow-draft flat-bottomed boat, they traveled together up the St. Croix River. The ice was melting quickly and the water was high as they struggled upstream. Foot-by-foot, the men fought the current all the way to Taylors Falls. The ground along the river was still covered in snow and the beaches were lined with ice. Around the clock they had to deal with rain and slush. The cold penetrated their clothes and even into their bone marrow. Several of the immigrants thought this was the worst part of the whole long journey from Sweden.

On April 23 the flat-bottomed boat finally arrived at Taylors Falls. Here the St. Croix River formed a great waterfall that blocked any further traffic upstream. The city consisted of six small block houses, two of which were joined together by a covered hallway to serve as a shop. A hotel would eventually be built in Taylors Falls, but there were no public accommodations for the Swedish immigrants. Somehow though they found a place to stay.

The men worked for ten days to widen the narrow Indian path to the lake so they could transport the luggage on horseback. At the shore of Ki Chi Saga the Swedes built some temporary housing. Wicklund built his north of the lake, and the others built east of the lake near today's Center City. The Wicklund family and brother-in-law Bylund soon decided they wanted to live more centrally and built a cottage two-and-a-half miles outside Taylors Falls. The Hälsinglander and the Östgötlander invested their future at lake Ki Chi Saga.

In June 1851, Anders Svensson sold fish to the monger in Taylors Falls and earned some well-needed money. Cajsa later worked at the hotel in Taylors Falls and was paid in sawn boards so her husband was able to build the first flat-bottomed boat in Chisago. Earlier the first settlers used hollowed-out logs when they wanted to go out on the lake to fish. The old technology from the Stone Age was still being used in Sweden to manufacture stock boats. In some regions they still used these boats into the early 20th century.

On July 21, 1851 Erik Norberg sent a letter from Ki Chi Saga to Pastor Gustav Unonius in Chicago. Norberg told him there was a Swedish settlement at the lake with 26 people, all doing well. At the end of the summer, Norberg received 50 dollars from the residents of Taylors Falls as a reward for successfully establishing a Swedish settlement at Ki Chi Saga. Then Norberg returned to his compatriots at Bishop Hill.

Anders Svensson assumed ownership of Norberg's property and built his cottage on a promontory on Norberg's island. The view of the lake was magnificent. The Östgötlanders cleared a small plot for vegetables and sowed the seeds they brought with them from home. A

1.1: *The stock boat at Attsjö school was manufactured in the early 18th century from a 300-year-old pine. The boat is 19 feet long and a little over 2 feet wide in the stern. The gigantic tree started growing on the outskirts of the village during Queen Margaret's[3] time. When "Stub-bakungen[4]" Henning Karlsson was living at Attsjö during World War II where he found a large number of stock boats. However, this well-preserved specimen was found 30 years later by two fishermen. In Attsjö this type of boat was used all the way into the 20th century. Photo: Bodil Stefansson.*

few weeks later Cajsa went to Taylors Falls with the kids on her back, and when she returned she found the deer had ravaged her garden.

As a dock worker in St. Louis Anders Svensson learned a little English. In the summer of 1851 this knowledge was valuable and he became a well-paid assistant to a surveyor. He earned almost $40.

In the fall of 1851 the settlers at Ki Chi Saga sent representatives to the Minnesota territorial legislature. The members wanted to replace the lake's Native American name. The Swedes advocated for Svensksjön (*Swede Lake*), which the English speakers were against. Finally, the name Chisaga was adopted, which after a typing error became Chisago. The settlers now lived in Chisago County.

Before winter the Swedes helped each other build timbered cabins that would withstand the wind and cold of winter. Joris Pelle bought a cow and a couple of oxen, one of which died. The neighbor Per Berg bought the other and constructed a primitive oxcart with solid wheels sawed by hand from an oak tree. He drilled a hole in the middle for the wooden axel, but the hole soon became an oval from bouncing over the impassible roads. The run-down wagon shook, jumped and squeaked, and the vehicle was named "screaming cart." The following year he rented it out for five dollars a day—to anyone who could afford it.

In August 1851 Anders Svensson wrote a letter to his relatives in the old country. A reply arrived three months later. On the fifth of January 1852 he sat down in the little dark cottage to write home again. Anders posted the letter at the general store in Taylors Falls, a 10-mile walk. The path was poor, the weather cold and the sky threatened a snow storm any minute.

Anders wrote to express his highest wish; that family and friends also would migrate and settle at Chisago Lake. He extolled life in America, but regretted that merchandise was so expensive and that the settlement lacked a priest. The United States was portrayed as the kingdom of heaven for women; "They do nothing but manage the home." All emigrants inclined to come to Chisago Lake were advised to travel through New Orleans—but were urged, "by all means guard your money, and let no one swindle it from you."

Gradually, the settlers at Ki Chi Saga began to realize the winters were harder and longer in Minnesota than at home in Sweden. The snowstorms were violent, came up suddenly and often lasted several days. Although it was no more than 300 yards to the nearest neighbor, Anders and Cajsa were completely isolated during a storm.

At dusk one cold winter evening the Svensson family saw forty wolves running across the ice directly toward their little house. On some nights the sound of loudly howling coyotes would infiltrate their home—reminding them they now lived in an isolated wilderness.

The earliest existing letter from Andrew Swanson [*Anders Svensson*] living at Chisago Lake is reproduced below in its entirety courtesy of the Archives of Svenska Emigrantinstitutet in Växjö, Sweden.

Chisago Lake (*Chisago läk*) January 5th 1852.

Dear dear siblings and brothers in law and sister in law and all your children and all friends whom I know. We thank you very much for the welcome letter I received with great joy on the 10th of November. Here I find that the heart of my brother still is warm and filled with love. I would rejoice to see you again and that I could expect you to come to this good country in the future, but it seems like I have to wait in vain. There is nothing I can do about that, but if you knew as much as I know, you soon would abandon your wretched country and go here. I hope that you will come here when I have been somewhat established and that the scene would be like when Josephs brothers came to Egypt, because here are all the good things a human being needs in this life. Here everything you sow and plant grows and here are one hundred sorts of good plants, so if we will be allowed to stay healthy and alive, here we will be able to live with few worries. Since we came here our health has been good, since the climate is sound and good at our lake, sjö (*lake*) is named "läk" here. We have excellent fishing here both winter and summer, which is good for all of us who have settled here. We are 16 men who have settled here, because we will believe that we be successful here. Next spring many will come from Iowa [*Jova*] because there the land is low and poor. Last summer there was a big flood, sweeping many houses away, something that often occurs there, so hence no one should go. All Swedes should go to Minnesota [*Minsota*], because here the climate is the same as in Sweden [*Sviden*]. We are kind of sad because we haven't got any pastor, but we have written a letter in order to get one next year. Every Sunday we gather and read a book of family sermons [*Postillan*] and celebrate the gospel of God and Jesus as well as we can, but when we will get more organized we will build a church. This might take another year, but thereafter I hope that everything will be both good and joyful.

Here up north everything sure is expensive and the reason for this is that the area has not been settled [*sätlat*] yet and nothing is for sale, since all goods go down to the states down south. But as soon as we have been established everything will work out just fine for us. One bushel [*busel*] corn costs one dollar [*daler*], one bushel wheat costs two dollars, one bushel potatoes costs one dollar, but the potatoes have the same disease here as in Sweden, one bushel rye costs one dollar, one bushel oat costs one dollar, half a pound [*1 mark*] pork costs 10 cents [*sänts*], half a pound of butter 25 cents. One dozen eggs costs 25 cents, half a pound of fish costs 10 cents. Here are many sorts of good fruits, but these are very expensive, since they are needed up in the Pineries. Up north 150 miles from here the loggers are cutting down very much timber for the sawmills. The logs are thrown into the river to be transported by the current and everybody makes a good profit. They pay you according to how much you can work, maximum 20, 25, 30 dollars a month and food for free.

I have been away working. During six weeks I was with a surveyor and I had 25 dollars per month and this was no hard labour. That much money I could not have been able to make in Sweden in a year. Even if they gave me 10 thousand Riksdaler (Swedish currency corresponding to 2500 dollars) I would not go back. Here a poor hardworking man is held in higher esteem than a rich man in Sweden and you are the same as anyone else. Both the poor and the rich and everybody is eating at the same table and do not have to be addressed by their titles. If you were to congratulate somebody the title of the male is Mister [*Mäster*] and the title of the woman is Mrs [*Mässes*].

You brother in law, Lars Jånsson in Österby, in your letter you are talking about that you would like to come here. If you do so, you are doing a good deed both for yourself and for your children. You ask what the best alternative would be. I think it would be to come where I am and take some land. Here is government land enough to last for 20 years, excellent beautiful and good land which you can cultivate for three or four years before you must make a payment. Since one acre can be bought for 1¼ dollars, a poor farm hand can get some land here. I have not paid anything as of yet and will not have to do so in some years. So if you come here you can at once start to cultivate your own land, I can guarantee you that.

And you, sister Anna Stina, wish to know what the working tasks of the women are here. Here the women do nothing, because they do not even milk their cows or carry in neither firewood nor water or spin or weave, because everything can be bought in the shop. Women never do anything more than cook food and do the laundry and sew for her own family, so America is excellently good for women. If a poor working girl comes here, in a month she will be dressed as well as the finest mademoiselle in Sweden, since a maid here earns 8 to 10 dollars a month if she knows the language. Thus if you my sister will come here alive and healthy, there is nothing more in the world you can wish for, that is for sure. Of course it is hard before you know some English, but you soon learn much enough to get by, especially the children learn fast, for grownups it is harder.

I wish to mention that the best way to go here is the way I travelled, because it is the cheapest and the easiest, but no ships depart until in the end of summer, which means that you will not arrive to America until it is winter. It is so hot in summertime (down south) so they can not sail there until it is winter. If you prefer to take that route, write to a man in Gothenburg. His address is Mr Kommersrådet O. Wik, but he will charge 100 Riksdaler (25 dollars) for grown-ups, half sum for children and those less than 3 years old go for free. If you write him, insist that you will not be charged anything while leaving the ship and say that you will be a big group, because the ship owners compete to get the passengers on their boats.

In the month of August I wrote you a letter wherein a map of the lake where we now have settled was attached. I am wondering if you got it. I also asked you if you are planning to go here. Do not believe that I am writing lies or that I promise you more than what is true.

I will take the sun and the moon as witnesses that every word is true. I hope that we have the one same God to guide us, though you are 8 hours before us in time; in winter the days here are 2 hours longer and in summertime 2 hours shorter. This winter has so far been cold with little snow, only 3 to 4 inches deep.

I would like to mention to you that you do not have to pay for any passport, toll or any other certificate, except for the one from the pastor (in Sweden). Here they do not ask you for any character or testimonial because this is a free country. Once in Gothenburg it will be enough to have what is mentioned above. The best way to change your money is to take a bill on board the ship you will travel on. They will give you 1 dollar for 4 Riksdaler.

It would be good to bring fishing tools, at least half a dozen of winter fishing lines of 12 fathoms, some good cordage for making fishing nets. Then you can bring some more small utensils according to your own desire, but do not bring any too-big trunks, because they are hard to lift. Big pots of copper are good to have here for cooking the fish. Bring some hemp weeds to test if it can grow here. Beware of your money and do not let anybody dupe it from you.

May the Lord give you manna thus you can come here and sow it and then eat it in a better land.

And. Svensson

My address is:
Mr. Andrew Swanson Minnesota [*Andro Svenson Minsota*]
Taylor Falls [*Täler fal Nordamerica*]
Native of Sweden [*Netil of Sviden*]

[Sve18]

2

How Magnus Jonasson emigrated from Linneryd and in North America wrote a long letter home

An early morning in the middle of May 1852, 17 people met at Åkerby junction[1] in Ljuder. Magnus Jonasson was the tall and authoritative leader. He left Kuppramåla in Linneryd parish along with his wife Lisa Stina Falk and four children. The emigrants made one last tearful farewell to relatives and friends. Magnus' oldest son Olof could not understand why everyone cried. For him it was a great adventure. Two participants, bachelor and farmhand Carl Jonasson, and Magnus' sister-in-law, servant girl Sara Helena Falk arrived from Hovmantorp. The other travelers came from Algutsboda and Ljuder.

In March 1852, the Wexjö-Bladet announced:
According to news from Ljuder in Konga härad[2] a significant number of parish residents have decided this year to move to the United States of America to cultivate a more fertile land than their homeland. The company of emigrants is said to consist of both old and young of both sexes and includes several healthy and enterprising youngsters. It is reported that some in the company have relatives in the Promised Land, who in detailed letters praised the happiness they had already found after their arrival.

2.1: *Magnus Jonasson. Photo: John Linn photo collection.*

Certainly, the last sentence refers to Magnus Jonasson's brother, Johan Linnell, who emigrated earlier in 1846. However, the rumors of the great emigration from Ljuder parish in 1852 were greatly exaggerated because most of people traveling with Magnus were from adjacent parishes. They merely arranged to gather at Åkerby Junction because it was a meeting point on the road to Karshamn. Several people who did receive exit certificates[3] from Ljuder had reneged. In the end only three people from Ljuder actually left for America.

Seven years earlier Ingrid Petersdotter from Bondeskog Södregård married the parish shoemaker in Ljuder, but her husband ran away before their son was born. Finally, Ingrid requested a divorce. From the pulpits in the churches of Konga härad clergymen demanded that the run-away-man return home within a year and a day. Now the divorce finally had been approved. Together with her son and brother, the "divorcée" was about to escape from the country in which this mark of shame would follow her through the church record books until she remarried, or until death if she remained single. Ingrid wanted to leave her shame behind, forget about the past and start a new life in America.

In Algutsboda parish, only one man was issued an exit certificate, but three men actually emigrated: Peter Svensson, Petter Johan Mattisson and Peter Magnus Jonasson Sjögren.

When Peter Svensson married in 1842, he became part owner of ⅜ mantal[4]. Two years later he was assessed 17 Riksdaler[5] in fines for highway robbery, fights and intoxication. Then it went rapidly downhill and in 1850 Peter and his family moved to become tenants in the old soldier croft in Östra Månsamåla. In the spring of 1852, he was issued an exit certificate to migrate with his nine and five-year-old sons, while his three-year-old daughter was allowed to move in with his parents. Peter was then 33 years old. His wife remained in Sweden and was recorded as a widow 15 years later.

Peter Magnus Jonasson, 34, also acquired ¼ mantal of Moshultamåla through marriage. He was born in the granary in Hällasjö where his father Jonas Sjögren was a farmer and a glassmaster. Peter also assumed the surname Sjögren. In May 1852 he left his wife Johanna and their five children to join the emigrants at Åkerby Junction. If North America was as good as its reputation, the rest of the family would follow the next year, which indeed came to pass. The author Vilhelm Moberg was born at Moshultamåla soldier's cottage in Algutsboda parish. During his childhood, storytelling was still practiced. His maternal grandfather's family had lived in Moshultamåla for generations. The maternal grandmother young Vilhelm fondly visited lived in the nearby Duvemåla. There her ancestors had lived and there she had her roots. Certainly, Vilhelm would have heard the stories about the first emigrants in the parish to leave for America.

Thirty-four-year-old Peter Johan Mattisson and his 12-year-old son left behind ¼ mantal of Mellangården in Västra Hällasjö. His wife Charlotta Jonasdotter stayed with their four-month-old daughter. Petter Johan left the parish without an exit certificate. During the forthcoming clerical household examination, the priest was irritated with the farmer for leaving without the priest's written consent. In America Petter took the name Kroon and was a member of the First Christian congregation when it was formed in Chisago County in 1854. When Petter Johan returned home after four years, he discovered that his wife had given birth to another child during his absence. Despite this, the family was reunited and two years later they had a son. During the famine of 1868 the husband and wife sold their farm and returned permanently to North America. Vilhelm Moberg's grandparents all lived in the Algutsboda parish and were all between nine and 23 years old at the onset of migration in 1852. But the fact that Peter Johan Mattisson's wife had given birth to a child in Karlskrona just before her husband came home after four years in America was never forgotten. A story such as this can be angled and twisted and give rise to much harmful, as well as mirthful gossip.

Magnus and his family lived just a mile away in Linneryd parish. In total there were 17 people, six from Linneryd, six from Algutsboda, three from Ljuder and two from Hovmantorp.

Vilhelm Moberg's emigrant characters gathered at Åkerby junction were 16 in number. There were two families, two farmhands, one single mother and a farmer who left his wife. Many comparisons have been made between these fictional emigrants and real people. Moberg himself said to his friend Gustav Lannerstock: "People ask how I used the material I researched · · · When the book is finished · · · I myself can't even separate poetry from reality."

In Karlshamn, Magnus Jonasson and his companions hired a sailboat with a crew of three men. They passed the Blekingian archipelago and rounded Skåne's sandy and treacherous south coast. In Öresund they encountered large ocean-going ships and small gaff-rigged fishing boats. The fields and pastures that extended to the horizon on either side of the strait were interspersed between fishing villages and towns. When the Vikings of the Baltic Sea sailed past Kullen a thousand years before, they made a sacrifice to their pagan gods to insure a safe and prosperous journey west. Now it was the provincial Småland farmers

2.2: *Moberg's 16 emigrants gathered at Åkerby Junction. From there, as true expatriates, they continued to Karlshamn by horse and wagon. Karl Oskar and Robert look forward, Kristina looks back. Photo: Ove Alström. (© 1971 AB Swedish Film Industry.)*

who sailed west. At the entrance to Kattegatt the straight widened and they passed Hallands Väderö.

The Halland coast was initially sandy and low, but when the boat approached Bohuslän, the land became more hilly and rocky. After seven days, the boat arrived at a dock in Gothenburg.

It took a full three weeks to find a good ship to sail the Atlantic. It was probably during that time that Magnus Jonasson befriended Matts Hansson[6] from Önnestad in Skåne. Matts' son Hans migrated to North America a year earlier in 1851 aboard the Swedish ship Ambrosius, along with a friend and some farmhands from Göinge. Several from this group pushed on farther westward to Illinois. From there they wrote to Matts Hansson that the country was fertile and the prospects were good. Now the fifty-year-old farmer was on his way to the American prairies. Matts from Skåne recommended that the Kronobergers sail with him aboard the Ambrosius, the same brig with a 12-man crew that Matts' son had taken a year earlier. Its skipper Captain Olsson was a highly honorable and recordable man. The Ambrosius was delayed four weeks before it finally arrived to load its cargo of pig iron. Bunks for 144 passengers had been built on a deck over the cargo hold, but the emigrants had to supply their own bedding and food.

After seven weeks of sailing, a fast transit at that time, the ship arrived in New York Harbor on August 3, 1852. There Hans Mattsson had been waiting one whole month for the Ambrosius to arrive. After a year in America, young Hans learned to write and speak English fluently. Now he would guide his father, brother and the other intrepid new immigrants further west to the city of Galesburg, Illinois. Many Swedes from Bishop Hill lived there. The soil in Knox County was very fertile but efficient transportation was not yet available and the farmers could not get their crops to market. Wages were low and many Swedes suffered from the harsh climate. They often were affected by chills and fever and were periodically bedridden and unable to work.

When Magnus Jonasson landed in New York, his older brother Johan Linnell was not there to meet him as they had planned. The party decided to stay a few days in case he showed up. They were overwhelmed by the crowds of people, diversity of languages and large houses in this big city. Here everything was for sale. Food aboard ship had been meager, but now it was difficult to resist the enticing fruits and the thick bright wheat bread baked with yeast instead of sourdough leaven. The Smålanders became sick with diarrhea and severe abdominal pain because their digestive tracts could not accommodate the sudden change.

Days passed and Johan Linnell failed to fulfill his promise to introduce them to a good country. Years later, Magnus and Lisa Stina's oldest daughter Ingrid Maria described her arrival In New York.

> Uncle Johan never showed up as promised, even though he had proclaimed in his letter to Magnus that he would have his American wife with him. "She is an American," he wrote. [Tud11]

Magnus Jonasson now realized that Johan had broken his word.

Thanks to the passenger list from the brig Ambrosius, we now know the Smålanders decided to travel to Illinois before they arrived in New York. But without Johan, they would not have the guidance he could have provided for the journey west via rivers, canals and lakes.

In Detroit, the new immigrants had to ride in a cattle car in which they were forced to sit on 8-inch wide boards laid on top of boxes.

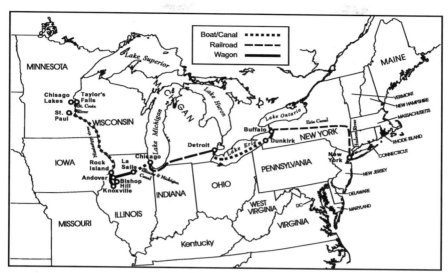

2.3: *Magnus Jonasson's journey from New York to Chisago Lake in 1852. Map: John Linn.*

Previously, the railroad car had been used to transport pigs. It had not been cleaned properly afterwards. When the train arrived two days later in Chicago, their clothes had absorbed the odor. In the station, "Yankees" stared disparagingly at the smelly pitiful immigrants. When the farm Kuppramåla was sold in January that year, Lisa Stina received part of her inheritance, which her husband managed. Magnus felt like a gentleman. With enough money in his pocket, he could provide for his family and buy tailor-made new clothes for the long journey. Now they were transported as pigs.

Back home in Småland, Magnus had always dressed well. On Sundays he used to wear silver buckles on his shoes while going to Church. As leader of the first emigrants from Kronoberg, Magnus Jonasson from Lambritsgård in Västorp finally filled the role he had long sought. In the new country, however, it was hard to feel like a leader. A person who could not speak the language was considered less knowledgeable.

From Chicago, the Smålanders went to La Salle via a horse-drawn canal boat. Then they continued by horse and wagon for two strenuous days and obtained accommodations in Andover, Illinois. A few days before they arrived twelve emigrants had died of cholera, but Magnus and his party of Kronobergers were not infected. The trip continued with a horse-drawn carriage ride to Knoxville. The men went out to inspect the fields, but they were disappointed because they did not want to live on a prairie without any forest. Then Magnus saw a copy of Eric Norberg's letter. In enticing words it described the fertile land around Lake Ki Chi Saga, where land sold for only a dollar and 25 cents per acre. In Knoxville the land was three times that much. The Småland farmers decided to follow Norberg's call and travel on to the Minnesota Territory.

During the boat trip up the Mississippi, Magnus and his company were relegated to the steerage deck where the emigrants sat with the cattle and the pigs. The food was poor and the deck was crowded. The trip took two weeks as the boat often ran aground on sandbars in the shallow river. Magnus' son Olof thought the sailors behaved like unruly animals when they took liberties with the women. The Smålanders clenched their hands in their pockets and wished they were back home. There they could defend a woman's honor. But now the men had to look on passively and felt humiliated. Initially the young girls were resigned, but not aunt Sara Helena, a big and strong woman. When one of the sailors approached, he was repelled with a powerful slap to his face. After that, she was left alone.

The immigrants landed in St. Paul, a city of 3000 inhabitants. The men in the company went on a reconnaissance trip on the Mississippi River, but found the land to be too sandy. Then Magnus Jonasson met a man named Rosell who owned land on Chisago Lake. He was willing to sell his new building and land for $100 and offered to accompany them to the lake as a guide. Magnus agreed. The company traveled by sternwheeler[7] to Taylors Falls. In the middle of the night, the captain dropped anchor below a steep rock that rose eerily from the water.

Lisa Stina had been through a lot since the time they first decided to emigrate. The farm where she raised her family was sold and she left her foster parents behind—never expecting to see them again in this life. One of her sisters was with her on the journey, but no one knew if any of her other siblings could come later. She did not expect to ever see her father again and her mother had been dead for many years. Seven weeks before she left Linneryd, Lisa Stina gave birth to a baby boy. Her body and mind had prepared her to nurse this newborn infant. But when baby Johan Peter died only ten days later, her milk-filled breasts became swollen and painfully tender. Because the Kyrktagning[8] had not yet taken place, Lisa Stina was not allowed to attend her son's funeral. Often a deceased infant was placed in a casket along with an adult. Probably, little Johan was buried beside the 75-year-old widow Sara from Barkabo Södregård in Linneryd, who was interred the same day—unless perhaps Magnus, in the midst of the task of preparing for emigration, had taken the time to hastily make a child's coffin for his son. The long journey from Sweden had been grueling, with sea sickness, starvation and overcrowding. Magnus's wife Lisa felt overwhelmed in this foreign country where the language was impossible to understand or speak. Through all this she had not complained, but when Lisa Stina awoke surrounded by the tall rocky cliffs and hills instead of the anticipated fertile fields and meadows, she said to her husband, "Are we finally coming to where you promised? The place where you do not need to dig rocks from the fields? Yes, thank you, it looks beautiful!" Then she burst out in tears for the first time in nearly five-months of travel.

Magnus had to pay five dollars for horse and wagon to carry the luggage from Taylors falls to the family's new home. It cost as much to haul the chests and suitcases these 10 miles as a man would earn from a full week's work in the woods. Because the road was poor and the carriage was brimming with the large immigrant chests, there was no room for anyone to ride. They took turns carrying three-year-old Eva, while six-year-old Martha had to walk by herself for most of the grueling trek. In October 1852, Magnus Jonasson's family arrived at Ki Chi Saga. Rosell had cleared four acres of land on Lönnö⁹ at the southern tip of Chisago Lake. The last occupant had started to build a small cabin, but this was far from finished and uninhabitable.

The previous winter the first settlers at the lake had slashed trees and brush to burn. But in the spring of 1852 it rained continually. Only when the weather improved in May could they burn the slashed brush so they could plant crops. By the end of the summer they would harvest rye, corn, vegetables and potatoes from between the stumps. Joris Pelle's wife (Carin Dannielsdotter) had planted flax and was the first at Ki Chi Saga to spin flax into linen threads.

In September 1852, the Swedes at Chisago Lake learned that there were four cows for sale in Marine Mills just over twenty miles away. A Dalslander had just moved there, but too late in the fall to find winter food for his cattle. Anders Svensson bought two cows for 30 dollars apiece. For all the families, milk was vital. Imagine his wife Cajsa's despair when one morning the cows were missing from around their

2.4: The landing at Taylors Falls. Photo: Ingvar Malmberg.

little cottage. She saw how the cattle had trampled the bushes and high grass and she followed the trail into the wilderness, unaware of where the journey took her. The only living creatures Cajsa might meet would be a wandering Indian or some wildlife, but she did not give up. She continued to follow the tracks for the rest of the day. In the evening, the tired woman met a man about 15 miles from her home. He had seen two stray cows several hours before, but could not find them now and feared Cajsa would get lost in the dark. But she dismissed his offer to spend the night at his campfire and continued her search, being given a couple of matches in case she had to camp out at night in the woods. Before it became completely dark, Cajsa found another building near Marine. To her great glee the owner had caught and corralled the cows she was looking for. It was 15 miles in a straight line back to Ki Chi Saga and significantly farther following the cows' path back home. The next day she returned the cows to her awaiting family. When this occurred, the energetic Östgötlander was seven months pregnant. Two months later, the first Swedish children were born in Chisago County; Both Cajsa and Joris Pelle's wife gave birth to daughters in late November 1852. [Hac90]

During the long journey from Åkerby junction to Ki Chi Saga, Magnus Jonasson had strengthened his conviction that he wanted to create a new Småland in North America. He felt mistreated by the Yankees and wanted to avoid contact with them. Instead, he wanted to get as many Kronobergers as possible to settle here. Magnus would then be able to converse with his neighbors in his native tongue and associate with people who shared his culture. The Swedish language should be spoken and Swedish values preserved in the church and in the soon-to-be-built schools. His dream was to be a wealthy landowner and have his close friends from Småland as neighbors. Next to his own homestead, he reserved land for Anders Peter Glader. The two would live as neighbors on the finest properties at the southern end of Chisago Lake.

Inspired by Norberg's circular, Magnus Jonasson wrote a letter to his brother Daniel in Tollstorp on October 26, 1852. In his long missive he indicated how it should be disseminated. Because this letter was readily duplicated, emigrant researcher Sven Adolfsson was able to obtain a copy more than 100 years later. Millions of letters would be sent across the Atlantic to Sweden. Most told of the immigrant's condition, everyday events and greetings. But Magnus Jonasson also described what he thought might be important for prospective emigrants to know and provided a detailed description of both what he had encountered and what he had left behind. In addition, we get a good window into the letter writer himself.

Below is the letter in its entirety. Clarifications by the author are in parentheses and punctuation has been added. Magnus was taught to read and write. He was known in Sweden as Big Writer [*Stor Skrivaren*].[10]

> Beloved parents and in-laws, as well as relatives and acquaintances, God be with you and all of us. The first thing I want to report to you is about religion and the worship service. As near as I can tell, religion here is revered more and considered more sacred than it is by you, though we have no church here yet, so we get together for our service and read and sing with a reading from a book of sermons.
>
> One month ago a Swedish priest (Unonius) visited and will return to us next summer. The priest here is paid

from a fund so that he is not allowed to beg from any of the congregation.

The soldiers here are only in the forts · · · a 5-year enlistment paid by the Government with clothing and food plus 100 dollars a year. The schoolmaster is given free land. That's his salary. Those who govern here are farmers who serve in terms (specific periods of time). Some of them receive a little salary.

Paid workers pay no tax, but if someone owns 100 dollars worth of livestock or similar assets he pays a tax of 50 cents. It's 100 cents to each dollar. Yet (this tax) still adds up to a lot of money in the treasury. In some of the earliest inhabited states there are many people who own 2–300 head of cattle and there were some who possessed over 1000 for which they could provide pasture and hay.

This country can never run out of land because it's rare that anyone owns less than 160 acres (1 acre = 0.87 Swedish acre) of land, and you won't find any crofters[11] or poor people scraping by in a backstuga[12] in America. And all the land that has not been surveyed or marked as land that can be sold may be used for harvesting hay by everybody.

Cattle and other livestock are expensive here because we are on the frontier with few people living here. For a couple of oxen it costs 60, 80 or 100 dollars but then they are quite large. A horse costs the same, a cow 25 and 30 dollars. It costs 1 dollar for a bushel of flax, wheat, corn and potatoes during spring time when it is the season to plant the potatoes. A bushel is 9 kappar (about 32 quarts).

But if you intend to buy a lot, you go down the river to Illinois [Elinos] or Iowa [Hjova Land] you can buy it for almost half the price.

When you've been here for a year and you have cleared away a lot of trees, you can at least sell your potatoes so you can take advantage of the high prices.

An unskilled laborer earns a dollar a day and usually plus food, you receive a higher salary · · · than in the southern states. Sjögren (one of the farmers from Algutsboda who joined Magnus party from Sweden.) worked for a month and received 16 dollars. Usually people who sign up for 1, 2 or 3 months are paid 20 dollars a month, a maid gets from 6 to 9 dollars a month. Both Sara Lena and Ingrid Christina got 6 dollars for the first month while they had no knowledge of the language, yet they did not harvest hay or any crops, nor pick up a single potato nor operate a spinning wheel or loom. They just cooked and kept house.

For one dollar I bought 10 yards of cotton cloth similar to linen. A yard is 3 feet and it was also a yard wide. The American foot is one inch longer than yours. In Sweden, there are about 50,000 square feet to the acre, but here it is about 45,000. The earth here is incomprehensibly fertile and bountiful. It consists of black soil with a layer of clay underneath and has no stones, with slightly hilly terrain, and the soil needs no fertilizers. Here we have a beautiful and fish-filled lake with several small lakes close by, so here even I can fish though I was an awful fisherman in Sweden. The wild game for hunting here consists of deer and birds. They are here in abundance.

Road maintenance is more or less non-existent. The new roads are being built by the Government. Those who live close to them do 2 days work a year but those who live 5 miles away have to repair their own roads. A Swedish mile is 6 miles here. The road tax is like your crown-tax.[13] There is no other tax for men, and women are never taxed.

Women have another advantage. If a girl testifies under oath that she was impregnated by a man and he does not want to marry her then he has to pay hundreds of dollars or work in a prison labor camp. Stealing is punished the first time and next time the thief will hang from the gallows, so · · · are no thieves here. This contrary to where you live. There most persons are brought up to adultery, stealing, falsehood and fraud and still you are warning others not to go to North America.

If you knew the low esteem with which your men in high places in society and your country are held, I am sure you would be coming here by the thousands and how you sin against a poor worker with a family to support and who might have to slave all day long for only 12 shillings a day. Here a worker has another benefit if he is a citizen or a new immigrant; he has the right to acquire 160 acres of land, and no matter how high a salary he has, still the soil will provide him an even higher income. Thus you understand that the soil is fertile. Payment for the land is rarely required until after 4 or 5 years and at that point you can pay for it yourself if you work hard.

Those without money can not manage more than 160 acres, but a person with cash can acquire an entire parcel consisting of 640 acres with all the lands at the same price. One and a quarter dollars per acre and here is plenty of land: all of the West and North is uninhabited, indeed half of America is still deserted. Here is no lack of land, only of manual labor.

You know the costs to cross the ocean, and on the railroad we paid 7 dollars per person to Chicago [*Cekago*], it is close to 200 Swedish miles, and when everything goes well it takes 2 days.

Crossing the ocean you can take as many things as you want, but on the trip you are limited to no more than 5 pounds per each adult person, and for any excess it's 2 dollars more for each pound, and not worthwhile. Take some heavy clothes, a few tools and copper pots, a lot of hand axes are unnecessary, a harrow [*plogskär*] ("Plogskär" probably describes an iron front edge for a wooden plow.) is better. You can put these iron tools in the bottom of a food box which is not weighed. A good American gun can shoot 300 yards.

Our trip went quickly from Chicago to Andover and from there we looped south to Knoxville. There we looked around. There were many Swedes, but the land was only plains (no forests) there, the heat was too much for us, and the earth is not as good as where we live now because of the blue clay underneath. There (in Illinois) the potatoes can grow OK, but here (in Minnesota) they thrive (like it very much).

From there we continued to the city of Chisago[14] [*Cekago*], where we traveled on the Mississippi River to the city of Galena and then to Saint Paul located in Minnesota Territory where we divided into two groups and went out to explore. We walked 10 Swedish miles and saw land of all kinds with land of grass in the wilderness, more than in all of Småland. It was a Swede named Ekman who said that we should buy flat land but that land was not to our liking.

There also was a Swede named Rossell whose home was where we now live. From there we journeyed to the town of Stillwater and from there to the town of Taylors Falls, which we now visit. We live one and a half Swedish miles (about 10 miles) west of that town.

Here we made a claim on woodland and forest consisting of oak, elm, maple and basswood,[15] some fruits of grapes, plums a kind similar to raisins and red gooseberries in abundance.

I paid for the work invested and the crops and gave Rossel 100 dollars. He had been a traveling salesman in Sweden. It worked out well since the price was good and I harvested enough hay for a couple of cows and it would not be any problem for me to provide hay for 100 cows.[16]

So that with the next fall and if it is the will of God I will harvest enough to support our household. Now we have finished buying what we need for the year.

So I'll show you a shorter way · · · From Chisago, the road is completed to Galena where you join the river and where you board a steamboat to Stillwater [*Stelwater*] and then to Taylors Falls [*Tälersfall*]. In Galena [*Galina*] you buy a chopping ax and a few other things you may need.

So this winter, you can write to Gothenburg to the ship-owner S. Liljeqwist at · · · a little west of the city, so you will get an answer from him and a promise to go on the brig if there is one and get the time when the ship leaves and if you do so, talk to Captain Olsson who commands the brig. Ask him about Magnus Jonasson. I promised him that I would recommend him to the people who follow me. It is unnecessary to make any down payment before you get there, because this is not a ride by horse and cart. Do not be too hasty to act and wait for a couple of days because if you want to take a different ship, you will lose your money.

We arranged with Liljeqwist to get handbills[17] and you must have the captain's receipt so you can get gold coins in New York. You will get a dollar and 3 cents for four Rd., perhaps 1 dollar and 6 cents · · · if you exchange them in New York · · · even if they are worth 2 Rd. all those silver coins are not worth it. Do not do it.

If you go with Captain Olsson, he is a most honorable and honest man. When you get on the train, you'll see how powerful it is, with 18 railroad cars behind the engine. There were 100 people, including our possessions. It traversed a Swedish mile in 10 to 12 minutes. Things here are done with machines; it is unbelievable; in Saw mills, flour mills. Chaff is removed from the grain, wheat is both sown and thrashed with machines. Some are powered by fire and some by horses and oxen. But when they need something chopped with an ax, then they like to hire a Swedish worker.

Churches here are rarely found outside of towns because it is a mere 1 or 2 miles between each town. Here there are some towns of only 8 or 10 houses. These houses are built from very thin sawn lumber. A proper house is built in 8 days and is covered with thin shingles. Here there are some birch trees so we can cover our roofs with birch bark.

Up here the river is very shallow and surrounded by high limestone cliffs and with sandy banks along the river. In the city of Galena lead can be found in the river banks so you do not need to bring it from Sweden. The land is useless on both sides of the river, and the boats turn here at the waterfall. The river is navigable from the city of New Orleans, 500 Swedish miles away.

Master masons are rarely used here. iinstead they use cast iron stoves, with appropriate pans and a baking oven, which is big enough for one household. It costs from 10 to 20 dollars. Brännvin (Swedish corn or potato spirits) is not sold in Minnesota but if someone wants to use it he may make it himself free of charge.

My property is located on the lake and is connected to the land on the south side and is altogether at least 100 acres and so I consider this much better than all 4 parts of Kuppramåla.[18] It is assuredly true that it requires a lot of work here in the beginning but after a while you get rewarded for the job done. The soil is loose after the forest has been cleared. And you plant with a hoe the first year, after that you can drive a harrow between the stumps because they are not closer together than the big stones in your fields, and praise the Lord, our health has not failed us one single day (we have been in good health).

The climate is much like southern Sweden but this land flourishes so well that we can get good quality grain. Here you will eat bread as least as good if you bought a cake at the baker's in town. Coffee and tea are used as are plenty of uncommon root vegetables that do not grow in your country. We immediately adopted the food customs here. Lisa and Sara Lena wish their sister Lena Cajsa would come here. People if you could help her to sail over the ocean, and maybe she could come in the company of someone who knew me who could help her out and then I would compensate them when they arrive.

If any of you are traveling here with plenty of money then 1 or 2 farmhands could come with you because I know you could have them work for a year to compensate you for their journey and then you would be pleased. The first year you will need them. He who comes here, be so kind as to bring a spinning wheel to my wife for payment · · · they are not used very often here, but will come in handy for making linen and yarn for knitting socks. The Swedes who settled here, get together to socialize but those who are not settled yet come and go.

It is not worthwhile for an upper-class couple to come here if they don't want to be farmers and don't understand how to farm. Journeymen will have problems making a living, except for a skillful and fast carpenter or a blacksmith, because it is done with machines better than you can imagine.

If you still have any supplies in New York then (continue) to use them in your journey through the country as the bread made in the city uses chemicals for fermentation that make you sick to your stomach. Do not eat much of the sweet fruit.[19] Glaziers are not needed here, because the glass is cut and is for sale in the cities. A town called Marine south of the falls is located as near to us as the Falls (Taylors Falls). We live at the south end of the lake. So the sooner you get here the better it will be for you to choose a good place because a man named Carlsson who comes from some place north of us in Sweden, has been sent out to find good land for a large number of people. I do not mean that you should hurry and leave earlier in spring than we did because the Atlantic Ocean is cold.

Brother Daniel apparently decided to stay because he does not believe he could find an equally beautiful or agreeable place in this country. I pity your poor slaves. However, if my father-in-law[20] was not married, I would have brought him too, but do not bring useless people who will be an annoyance to you if you help them to get a job, because the American has a fiery temper. Surprisingly, he does not work both day and night but half the day to work and half to rest and yet smokes his pipe during the day. Tobacco is plentiful · · · it grows well, but snuff is seldom used.

A shoemaker or tailor would be handy for us but he should also be able to do unskilled labor. For the American buys his clothes ready made and the women do all the sewing themselves. Shoes and boots are mended in the store. A pair of boots cost 2, 3 or 4 dollars and the heavy ones are the best in the price. I do not have time to write more this time and I must stop. I promise tailor Andreas from Ljuder who sewed my clothes with your skill, you can not make much money here but if are willing · · · as a laborer, come here. I can shelter and feed you until we can recommend you to someone who will give you a job.

Farmhand Carl Jonasson from Linnehult who came with me also has taken land because it does not matter if you are poor. Now he works in the woods[21] for 3 months, so he can earn 60 dollars.

Let me know how thing are going in Black Sweden[22] with my parents who are too old to come but my wife's parents in Vide[23] would not have regretted it if they had come here · · · but please have mercy and help Lena Cajsa Falk · · · my brother-in-law you can come and I'll get you a better place · · · I think the trip worthy to you and your children[24] · · · but do as you please. Now I have described what I currently know. Both Lisa Stina Jonasdotter and Sara Lena Jonasdotter and our family and the other Swedes thrive here and are very well. This is a good place for young women, if they want to marry or serve.

Here is my address: [*Här har ni adressen:*]
Farmer [*Farmannen*] Magnus Jonasson
Chisago Lake [*Cekagolek*]
Taylors Falls, Minnesota [*Tälersfall, Mennessotta*]
North America [*Nord Amerika*]   [Ad090]

Magnus Jonasson chose to omit the fact that the former owner Rosell had not yet completed the crude dwelling, and it was thus uninhabitable. On the other side of the lake stood the pioneer Per Wicklund's first ramshackle cabin measuring 12½ by 13 feet plus a porch on one end. The inner roof was missing and the roof was made from partly cracked elm bark. When it was snowing, someone had to get up on the roof and sweep the snow away otherwise it would melt and drip into the room. Magnus' family stayed in this cabin, along with Peter Svensson from Algutsboda and his two sons, nine and five years old. Six beds were crowded together with a carpenter's workbench that the men used to make beds, tubs, buckets, benches and other household items. Beneath the roof, wet clothes hung on a line to dry. Lisa Stina was forced to manage the household of nine people. During the cold winter, the fire had to burn around the clock so the frost would not penetrate the cabin. Son Olof was assigned to keep the stove lit and to gather fuel from the forest. The snow was deep and the 13-year-old thought he had a difficult task.

When spring came, Magnus finished the cabin that Rosell had begun so they could live on the peninsula Lönnö. During the summer he built a sturdy 20 by 30 foot Småland style timber house for his family. Thanks to the fact that the previous owner had cleared four acres of land, Lisa Stina and the children could plant potatoes the first spring they lived at Chisago Lake. With the help of wooden hoes, they dug up 100 bushels of potatoes and that autumn the crops were harvested and buried underground to keep them free of frost. The surplus would be sold in May of the following year, hopefully for one dollar per bushel.

In 1853 Peter Svensson from Algutsboda bought 200 acres of land for 250 dollars and settled south of Little Lake with his two sons. In 1853, his three-year-old daughter left Sweden with the family of Sven Magnus Petersson from Rävemåla, and joined her father and brothers. A total of 30 people from Algutsboda arrived that fall. Peter sold his 200 acres to his relative Sven Magnus the following year and moved to a small new building on a peninsula on the southern part of Little Lake. To the north of the lake lived Håkan Larsson Swedberg. This Swede from Bleikinge had a strict Christian faith and became a vanguard of the Lutheran community. Surely he had many heated discussions with Peter Svensson, who never joined any church and had a bad reputation in the old country

In 1853 hundreds of Kronobegers emigrated to America. Many of them arrived in September in Chisago and Washington Counties and become settlers. Autumn was almost over, the weather was getting cooler and the chilly October winds blew strong, but the Glader family had not yet arrived. Every day, Magnus and Lisa Stina became increasingly worried. What had happened to Anders Peter, Elin and the seven children from Berget in Västorp?

3

How Carl from Linnehult took the name Linn and walked 300 miles to buy cows

It was widely known in Furuby that Maria Petersdotter was the grand-child of the rich juror Israel Jonasson from Västorp and was the second cousin of Anders Peter Glader. In a society where everything was organized through bloodlines and personal contacts, most people in the community were able to describe their family relations back four or five generations. Maria grew up at Amundsgård in Västorp and in 1824 married Jonas Andersson from Näsby in Dädesjö parish. The couple moved to Hovmantorp and bought a small farm in Klintalycke. There twins Carl and Cajsa were born. In 1833, Jonas and Maria moved to nearby Linnehult Södregård occupying ¼ mantal.

Supporting a large family of nine children required several different ways of earning money. During the winters in the1840s, Jonas, with the help of his sons, collected bog-iron ore from lake Rottnen. The ore was laying on the bottom and was scooped up and fished through a hole in the ice while they gladly stood behind a windscreen.

They were paid 10-16 shillings per barrel, depending on quality. The best was the pearl ore which gave an additional two shillings per barrel. Jonas earned the most money in 1835 when he received a credit for 24 Rd. in return for 122 barrels. The Lessebo iron factory preferred to make payment in goods so Jonas Andersson usually received his compensation in bar iron, rail iron, shovels and plowshares, items that he could use for trade.

The children at Linnehult Södregård were each confirmed at the age of 15, but did not need to go out and serve until they were around 20 years old, suggesting the farm was sufficiently prosperous to sustain the family. The oldest son Carl worked as a farmhand for a total of four years, first at Ormeshaga Fiskaregård[1] and then in Linneryd. When the sons of Linnehult Södregård had become old enough, they transported timber to the seaside towns during the wintertime. Many years later Carl Linn told the neighbor boy at Chisago Lake about something weird, which happened one night in the old country:

32

3.1: *The model was made by Göran Eriksson and now belongs to Hemmesjö Hembygdsförening (Hemmesjö Community Association). Photo: Ingvar Malmberg.*

My brother and I were driving lumber from Linnehult in Hovmantorp parish to Karlshamn. We were driving at night. It took three days because we only had one horse. Many times when we drove past churches and graveyards my brother saw things that I could not see. Once when we drove past a graveyard the horse began to labor very heavily under the load. Then my brother came up to me and said:

"Kalle, be quiet... Say nothing! There are two small gnomes riding on my load, and the horse is pulling so hard he is working up a sweat."

"Just be quiet," I told him.

Then we came to a Church and he said: "Now they went away... now they left and went into the church."

And then the lights were on in the Church! It must have been some kind of witchcraft... the gnomes left the load, went in to church and it was lit up... and there was no one in the church at that time—two o'clock in the morning!

In 1851 Carl Jonasson was 25 years old and engaged to be married. He found the woman in his life but did not know how to provide for a family. The woman Carl wanted to share his life with was named Lena Cajsa Falk. She was 21 years old and worked as a maid at Thorsjö manor in Östra Thorsås. Her older sister Lisa Stina would soon emigrate with Magnus Jonasson and their four children from Kuppramåla in Linneryd to North America. When Carl was invited to go along, he did not hesitate.[2] On a very early morning in mid-May 1852, the entire household of Linnehult Södregård was up and about. The horse was harnessed and the heavy travel chest was loaded onto the cart. Carl's younger brother Johannes took the reigns while Carl sat down beside the driver. After a last farewell to his parents, the eldest son left the home—never to return. The emigrants converged at the junction at Åkerby. Together they all continued on toward Karlshamn. 17-year-old Johannes returned home to Linnehult, unaware that he had just seen his future wife for the first time.

By the mid 1800s, a trip by sailboat from the European continent to North America took an average of eight weeks with fair wind and following seas. In Gothenburg, the company of emigrants boarded the sailboat Ambrosius and on the 5th of August 1852 the ship arrived in New York. Even though the trip took only seven weeks and two days, it had been stressful, especially for all those who had brought too little food with them. More than 100 years later Carl Jonasson's grandson told how his grandfather nearly starved on the boat. The three weeks waiting in Gothenburg must have consumed a lot of the food reserved for the trip.

The Smålanders arrived at Ki Chi Saga in early October 1852. During the first winter, Carl worked for 20 dollars a month in the tall pine forests 100 miles to the north, most likely in a forest lumber camp along the Rice River.

Southwest of Magnus Jonasson's new home was a beautiful elongated lake, later named Linn Lake. Carl decided to settle between the shores of Linn Lake and Chisago Lake. His greatest wish was the people closest to him also would immigrate and settle next to him. With the help of his neighbors, he built a small cabin to accommodate his fiancé and his siblings when they arrived. Like many other immigrants to America, Carl changed his last name and chose the surname Linn. Family stories say he took the name from "Linnehult," his family home in Sweden. "Linn" is the word for "linden tree" in the old Småland dialect spoken at the time of his immigration.[3] At home at Södregård in Linnehult there had been a lot of linden and ash trees, the leaves of which had been harvested and used for winter fodder for the animals. Linnehult means "thicket of linden trees" which describes how the surroundings once looked. Still today there are huge old linden trees in the yard and old gnarled stumps of ash trees still stand.

In the spring of 1853, Jonas and Maria from Linnehult Södregård lost another five children to American emigration. Peter, who was 22 years old, became the foster father for the group. Johanna, 25 years old, took on the role of the mother, cook, trustee of the food and caregiver for the others, especially when they got sick. John, 19, had been told to be guardian for his little sisters, Ingrid and Lena, who were 15 and 12, respectively. For the parents who remained in Sweden, it was comforting that the youngsters were sailing with their uncle Johannes and his large family from Ugnanäs in Hovmantorp parish. Also, Carl's fiancé Lena Cajsa Falk had managed to make enough money for a ticket and joined the company.

On July 3, 1853 the sailing ship St. Patrick left Liverpool, entering New York Harbor on August 15 after sailing only six weeks. In September, the siblings arrived at Chisago Lake and settled into the tiny cottage Carl had built. Their mother's brother Johannes, who had come to America with them, settled with his family in Washington County just to the south. Several other families from Hovmantorp parish also accompanied them to Chisago Lake.

Lena Cajsa and Carl were engaged before Carl ventured to America. Now they wanted to get married as soon as possible, but at Chisago Lake there was no church and rarely a priest. And in 1855 when a cleric appeared without notice, Carl was not at home. After a lot of running here and there, the groom was found out in the woods. They were married, but there was no time to dress up or to arrange a wedding party. Lena Cajsa explained 50 years later that the newlyweds were very poor, but that it was a joy to share the same pillow. [Tud11]

For the new families in Minnesota, cows were as important to survival as they were for the crofters back home in Småland. Here on the frontier, animals were expensive and a cow cost $30. A good dairy cow in Småland could be purchased for the equivalent of $8. The poorest Minnesota pioneers could not afford to buy either cows or oxen. In 1853 Carl Linn and two other Smålanders went down the Mississippi River by paddle steamer to the city of Galena, Illinois. Cattle prices there were a lot lower. After buying some dairy cows, the men walked home on a journey of about 300 miles. In places where there was plentiful grass the cows could graze while the men drank milk. [Ber81]

In the early years of Chisago Lake, the newcomer's cattle were free to roam in the woods during the summer. Some days Lena Cajsa had to search for a long time before she found them. After the two cows had been milked, she had to shoulder the yoke and carry the buckets of milk home over the shoddy trail without splashing the milk out of the buckets. Sometimes the cattle had walked far away. Several times when it was rainy and foggy, Lena Cajsa got lost on her way home . . .

Carl Linn told the neighbor boy Arvid about the first difficult years:

> Deer and fish were plentiful, but we needed to purchase salt and flour and many other things. Then, I had to carry all the supplies back from Stillwater, Marine Mills or Taylors Falls. Our only guide was a trail we blazed on the trees as we went. Sometimes I carried as much as one hundred pounds along with my gun at my side. And then I had to sit puffing alongside the road. After a few years, we grew all that we needed, but it was hard work going into the wilderness to clear a small field for cultivation in a forest with trees standing together as close as rye in a field. For example, it took two to three years before I could grow my own potatoes. At first, it was virgin forest with a log hut here and there. At that time I could never imagine that all forests would be cut down and that all lands would become fertile fields.
>
> [Car62]

When Carl's grandson, George Noren, reached 105 years old, he told some Swedish folklore researchers that the settlers felled trees and burned the branches to fertilize the fields before they sowed the rye. They harvested it with a sickle and carried the shocks in bags, but they had to wait to thrash the grain until there was ice on the lake. Then the men carried the grain on their backs seven miles to the mill in Franconia. Boiled porridge and baked bread were made from the flour. [Ber81]

Most of the settlers at and around Linn Lake at the southern part of what is now South Center Lake had roots in Dädesjö, Furuby and Hovmantorp parishes. Magnus Jonasson had finally realized his dream: to

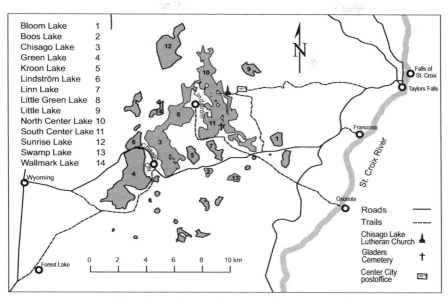

Bloom Lake 1
Boos Lake 2
Chisago Lake 3
Green Lake 4
Kroon Lake 5
Lindström Lake 6
Linn Lake 7
Little Green Lake 8
Little Lake 9
North Center Lake 10
South Center Lake 11
Sunrise Lake 12
Swamp Lake 13
Wallmark Lake 14

Roads
Trails
Chisago Lake
Lutheran Church
Gladers
Cemetery
Center City
postoffice

3.2: *Roads and trails at Chisago Lake. Map: John Linn.*

create in America a community in which the language of the homeland was spoken, the old culture was maintained and where he could live surrounded by his old friends from Kronoberg county.

After a few years, these Smålanders would break away from Chisago Lake Township and instead align themselves to the south. Due to the spread-out nature of Chisago Lake, it was difficult for a country road to reach Chisago City and Center City. New settlers wrote a petition saying that it would be much easier for them to conduct most of their many business deals and transactions in the city of Wyoming. The petition was signed by 33 Swedish men, most of them from Kronoberg county, who claimed that section 24 of Township 33, Range 20 would join the Wyoming Township. Carl Linn was the first to sign the letter, indicating that he had been a key sponsor of this issue. The proposal was approved and was implemented in 1858.

Many of the early emigrants to Chisago County came from Kronoberg county. Several of them who settled near Carl Linn's brothers were either related to the Linn family's mother Maria Petersdotter or to their father Jonas Andersson. It began to feel like home.

*Maria Petersdotter from Amundsgård[4] in Västorp
and Jonas Andersson from Näsby[5] in Dädesjö
became the link between the two family groups
that first settled at the southern part of Ki Chi
Saga, later called South Center Lake. At Linnehult
Södregård, Maria and Jonas raised nine children.
Eight of them emigrated to North America, while
the youngest daughter Emma married and stayed
in Sweden to care for her aging parents. Seven of
her eight children eventually emigrated to
America as well. [Lin]*

3.3: *Maria Petersdotter & Jonas Andersson.
Photo: John Linn collection.*

*John Linn in the ancestor's cottage. Note that
the doorway to the living room does not even
reach the height of his chest.*

3.4: *John Linn in his ancestor's cottage.
Photo: Ingvar Malmberg.*

*The old residence from Klintalycke was moved to
hembygdsparken (Hovmantorp Community Park)
in Hovmantorp. The room on the left has been
removed, but the living room, the vestibule and
the utility room still remain. The doors are low,
the windows are few and the windowpanes are
small.*

3.5: *The ancestor's cottage from Klintalycke.
Photo: Ingvar Malmberg.*

4

How Glader emigrated with his family and followers and about the ship's Atlantic crossing with damaged rigging, lack of water, starvation and death

In the fall of 1852, Anders Peter Glader made new emigration plans with his neighbor Nils Håkansson at Nilsagärde. The men decided that together with their families they would emigrate to Ki Chi Saga the following spring. Lisa Stina, who was Nils' wife and Glader's cousin, vehemently opposed the men's plan. She possessed a strong will and was not afraid to say "Go ahead—but the kids and I stay!" Nils tried to convince Lisa Stina to go with him to Minnesota, but his wife, his senior by five years, was immovable. The family finally remained in Småland, purchasing the Glader homestead Berget for 2,600 Riksdaler:

> This day we approved the transaction and sold the farm we have owned until now consisting of ⅕ mantal (old definition) now changed to ³⁄₄₀ mantal (new definition) of Wästorps Lambritsgård in Furuby parish located in Konga judicial district to Nils Håkansson and his wife Lisa Stina Johannesdotter from Nils Gärde for the agreed purchase amount of 2,600 Riksdaler. A debt agreement for the sale has been paid and thus the transaction has been completed and in accordance we relinquish the right of ownership and will allow the buyers to occupy the dwelling next fardag[1] March 25, 1853, including soil, land, meadows, forests and fields in their present condition, and it can be used by the buyer without any further court hearing or need for a court order for this purpose. This declaration is signed in front of witnesses present in Wästorp this 4 January 1853.
>
> Seller: Anders Peter Nilsson, Elin Svensdotter.

The Glader family made many preparations for the trip. Anders Peter bought over 300 feet of iron strap from Lessebo forge[2] to strengthen the many wooden chests he constructed. The family needed sturdy luggage for clothes, bedding, equipment, household accessories and food that must be stored for a long time. Often the early emigrants had to provide their own food during the long sea voyage across the Atlantic. To ensure enough they were advised to bring aboard enough for 12 weeks. For Elin it must have been difficult to know how many provisions to take because the length of the journey was conditioned on the weather. In addition, the food had to include the trip to Gothenburg and any waiting period before the ship departed.

Today it is difficult to get a clear idea of how big Glader's food box was and what it contained. The farmer Andrew Peterson of Carver County maintained a diary for 30 years, to the great benefit and delight of Vilhelm Moberg. But neither Glader's wife Elin nor Magnus Jonasson's wife Lisa Stina could write or keep a diary. The women were responsible for the food while the men wrote the letters home. No women in a farmhouse in Furuby or a Swedish homestead at Chisago Lake kept a diary in the 1850s. The concept was alien to them. However, using the available written sources, we can conclude that the food the Glader family brought with them for the long journey to Ki Chi Saga consisted of salted, smoked and dried meat, probably sausage and cheese and baked rye bread and rusks that Elin baked just before leaving. Anders Peter drove to the gristmill to grind grain used for making barley porridge. Whether Elin brought herring, potatoes, peas, sugar, onions and coffee is less clear. They packed schnapps and possibly vinegar to be used for medicinal purposes. Contemporary accounts describe kegs of beer and sour milk lashed to the bunks on the middle deck. In addition, the family needed to bring aboard a bucket for the daily water ration, a cooking pot, spoons to eat and a knife to cut bread and meat.

In the month of March 1853 everything they didn't take with them went under the hammer in an auction at the farm Berget. At the end of April 1853, Anders Peter Glader acquired a transit certificate for his family of nine people. His sisters Cathrina and Helena and two farmhands also joined the party of emigrants.

More than 100 years after A. P. Glader emigrated, Oskar Johansson from Berget was interviewed by the emigrant researcher Sven Adolfsson. Oskar's grandmother Lisa Stina told Oskar that her cousin Anders Peter was a skilled workman in both farming and carpentry—but she added: "Glader was a little unstable. The people around him thought he was awfully stupid to have moved. He had no problems with any-one here but "det var aldrig tillräckligt gott" (*"but it was never good enough"*).

In Gothenburg in the summer of 1853 a former sheet-metal worker [*plåtslagare*] named Jonsson started booking emigrants to go to North America. His prices were favorable. For 100 Rd. they could take a route by steamer first to Liverpool and from there travel by fast packet ship to New York. Anders Glader and family were one of the 200 Swedes who purchased tickets, and they thought it was a good deal. The emigrants themselves were to provide their own food for the four-day-long trip to England and then all supplies would be included aboard the boat to New York.

On Jonsson's advice, Glader relinquished all their excess food and beverages. In Liverpool Mr. Jonsson guided the Swedes to the big En-glish packet ship that was to carry them. Packet ships were built to quickly transport parcels and mail. Some captains did not receive a fixed salary, but instead were paid a percentage of the value of what they were shipping. The ships embarked according to a fixed schedule and were sailed without regard to passengers or crew.

Six hundred emigrants from Ireland, England, Germany as well as Sweden were packed into the middle deck, where the ceilings were low and ventilation was poor. Before boarding the Franklin King, the purser asked Glader for his name, age, nationality and occupation, but he did not speak Swedish and none of the Swedes spoke English. Glader chuckled to himself when he was asked about his occupation. He did not answer "farmer" like most of the others but joked instead and said in his broad Västorp dialect: "Ja e låjer," (*I am ugly*), know-ing fully well that only the Smålanders would understand. His rep-utation as a practical jokester was written in stone when the similar English word "lawyer" was recorded as his profession, probably the only Swedish lawyer going to America in 1853.

Of all emigrant ships departing from Liverpool the conditions on-board the English ships were the worst; where poor emigrants were packed tightly in the smallest possible space. There was a galley on deck where they cooked their food. The wood fired cooking stoves[3] [*eldstäder*] were few and bickering and quarrels were a part of every-day life aboard. Women who were not tough enough did not get a turn or were pushed away before their food was cooked. Here everything was ruled by bullies.

In an article of February 25, 1854 the newspaper *Folkets Röst* (*People's Voice*) from Kalmar lamented "Warning to emigrants!" The author was Gustaf Hällgren who lived in Jamestown in New York State. "My Christian love and duty and my aversion to every dastardly deed, invite me to present the following facts to all Swedes. Warning to emigrants! And shame to the deceptive man."

The information came from Gustaf's cousin Hans Gårdman, who emigrated from Lönneberga parish. Among the many names from the Franklin King's passenger list, John Everett Jones identified about 60 Smålanders from the following parishes: Furuby, Gårdveda, Järed, Karltorp, Kråkshult, Lönneberga, Målilla and Södra Vi. From the newspaper article we can confidently surmise that the ship at the center of this atrocity was the notorious Franklin King.

People from four different countries were crammed together into the middeck. According to Hans Gårdman, the Irish were sloppy, dirty, and a pack of thieves—and they generated most of the arguments and fights. Starting the very first night, many Swedes were robbed. Eventually mistreatment occurred in broad daylight and theft was not even concealed. No one dared to intervene. Every day the Swedes were pushed and struck, but they could not complain to the captain because none of the Swedes spoke English. They were completely powerless against the rough sailors. [Jon]

Worst of all, the promised plentiful food was not to be. Hans Gårdman estimated the weekly ration as 3.5 pounds of bread, 5.5 cups of oatmeal, 3 cups of rice flour and some tea and a little sugar. That is a total of only 7,000 Calories for two adults and one child to last for one week—only a fifth of their total energy needs. After three weeks of this kind of starvation, total fatigue and apathy occurs and generally adults become bedridden after four weeks. Eventually many of the body's organs stop working. After nine weeks of such extreme starvation usually 60% of the victims would die. [Soc00]

Hans Gårdman was at a loss for words to describe the suffering the famine caused, but what struck him as the most heartbreaking was what happened during the food distribution—where the small starving children sought to grab the hard bread crusts spread on the deck and how the mean and heartless sailors then beat them on their fingers. With every day, the Swedes became more and more feeble. It was incomprehensible how anyone could survive solely on this puny ration. At first, the weakest women and children became bedridden. Everyone languished and eventually even the strongest men could barely support the weight of their own body—and then it got even worse.

On August 5th, the Franklin King was at 41° 58' north 52° 30' west and making good time with all sails unfurled. Two-thirds of the distance had been covered and they were passing the Grand Banks of Newfoundland when a powerful squall suddenly appeared out of the west-southwest. With a terrible noise, the three topmasts broke near their caps and went overboard with the sails and riggings, the jib-boom was lost and the mainyard was carried away, the mainsail and the foresails split and the foreyard was damaged. For four days, the ship rode out the storm with only the foresails and the crossjack. [Jon]

Originally estimated to be four weeks, the trip was stretched by another three weeks and the Franklin King finally arrived in New York on August 26th. Gustaf Hällgren attributes the death of no less than 22 Swedes onboard to the extended delay and starvation at sea. More died after landing in America. Others were immediately sent to a hospital, where even more died, and some passengers were so weak they had to remain in New York. Hans Gårdman was sure that none of the Swedes would have survived if the trip had taken another two weeks. He believed the worst part of this heinous act was having plenty of food on board, but yet not allowing anyone to buy any of it. On the ship's passenger list, all who died were Swedes. The companies that chartered German and English immigrants knew rations on board were limited and therefore they provided their passengers with enough barrels of food to last the entire trip. The Swedes were now convinced that Mr. Jonsson from Gothenburg, who had ventured over the Atlantic several times, knew that it was impossible to survive on the ship's minimal rations. Yet, he found the cheapest ship, appropriated and sold the food they brought for the journey across the Atlantic, and then stuffed the extra profit into his own pocket. The survivors hoped that this villain and fraudster would suffer every curse his murdered compatriots had uttered about him up to their last dying breath.

Gustaf Hällgren's article points out that for those who survived the terrible sailing aboard Franklin King, the memory of this tragedy would never go away, but it would diminish quickly over time. Hällgren did not think it likely they personally would write to newspapers describing their experiences and warning others. Most of the Swedish passengers could not write and those who could were so busy dealing with their own suffering that they could not worry about others.

Therefore, Hällgren set out to do everything in his direct power to make Mr. Jonsson's criminal deception publicly known. In this way he hoped to prevent more emigrants from starving to death. In the summer of 1853, another nine Swedes died on a different ship after being deceived by the same Mr. Jonsson. In New York, Gustaf Hällgren sent his letter about the voyage of the Franklin King to Gothenburg's *Handels och Sjöfartstidning* (*Trade & Shipping*) magazine, but feared that the newspaper would not publish his letter owing to conflicts of interest and excessive competition for column space.

Many years later Anders Peter Glader's grandson Irving Quist told the story of his mother Sofia's voyage over the Atlantic Ocean in 1853—a trip so horrible that it was impossible to describe.

> When the Franklin King was merely 100 nautical miles off New York's Long Island, the ship was hit by a tornado. All the masts and the sails went overboard. For three days whenever the ship dropped into the trough of a wave, the passengers were convinced that the Atlantic waves would swallow them—but the hull remained intact. Many of the water barrels in the cargo hold were broken or began to leak. During the next three weeks, water was restricted and many of the children died.

The Glader family arrived in New York four-and-a-half months after they left home. The passenger list indicates 15 out of 43 children aboard the ship died. All were from Sweden. Glader's two-year-old daughter Petronella was one of them. It might have been from either starvation or dehydration. [Blo06]

During the last weeks of the trip the Swedes were in such poor condition that breastfeeding mothers could no longer produce milk for their babies. Vulnerable from lack of fluids and without breast milk, the small infants were first and foremost to die. We do not know if the water barrels were really so totally depleted or if Sofia's story was a way to obfuscate what really happened: theft, abuse, humiliation and starvation.

Those who have been abused and exploited often feel ashamed; shame from being humiliated in front of others; shame from seeing their family humiliated; shame from being so easily duped; shame from being treated as a second-class human being and feeling a destructive self-contempt from the inability to stand up for themselves or their children. This is not something you reveal but just try to move on and forget. Children exposed to tragedy may not even remember what actually happened—only the feelings remain.

When the tornado struck, Glader mistakenly thought the Franklin King was close to the American coast because by then they had been sailing for several weeks. But Anders Peter had no means to know their true position. In reality the ship still had a thousand more miles to go. The crew didn't speak Swedish so they couldn't tell him, nor any other Swede, where they were or what was happening—and it is not likely the crew would have said anything even if they could. The emigrants were kept in the dark, feeling as if they didn't matter and further heightening their sense of isolation and helplessness. Hans Gårdman claimed the Swedes never knew the name of the ship they sailed on—but Anders Glader knew the name Franklin King well, and probably so did all the Swedes. Perhaps Gårdman needed a ruse to avoid making the Franklin King public to protect the Swedish victims from being identified and facing further shame—allowing them to aim their pride forward toward the new land and leave their humiliation behind at sea.

Not all emigrants treated poorly during the North American crossing were silent about their experiences. In the summer of 1853, 14 Norwegians wrote a Norwegian newspaper about their trip to New York aboard an English packet ship.

> The bunks onboard were full of lice. Substandard food was thrown to the emigrants as if they were dogs. Then the crew laughed as fights broke out amongst the Norwegians. The women could not protect themselves from the seamen and the men were beaten when they did not understand orders barked in English. On arrival in New York, several of the passengers had facial injuries, missing teeth and broken ribs. Others were so weak they could not stand due to lack of food.   [Ble41]

From New York, The Glader family continued on west by boat, train, and horse and buggy. Glader's four-year-old daughter Lovisa Fredrika had survived the voyage to America, but she had no reserves left. When the family arrived in Chicago, the girl was dead. After the funeral, the horse-drawn journey continued to the Mississippi River and on September 29 they arrived in St. Paul. The final leg of the trip was by steamboat up the St. Croix River. On one side was Minnesota

Vilhelm Moberg was fascinated by the St. Croix's "Old Man of the Dalles" because he thought it resembled an Indian and so in his book he placed the stone figure at Ki Chi Saga instead. In the Moberg Archives at the Emigrant House in Växjö there are postcards, photographs and enlargements of this peculiar rock formation. St. Croix Falls in Wisconsin is in the background.

4.1: *Old Man of the Dalles.*
   Photo: Ingvar Malmberg, Graphics: John Linn.

Territory and on the other the state of Wisconsin The closer to their destination they were, the landscape became more rock strewn and more crags lined the river. Sometimes the immigrants were afraid they would run aground when they saw how shallow the clear water was as it flowed over gravel and rocks, but the paddle-wheeler continued steaming on by.

Trees with trunks many feet in circumference stood out against the sky. For the last half hour, the river was surrounded by tall cliffs with large stone blocks and ledges. Here in the rocks they could see the holy cross that gives the river its name and the face of an old man. In Taylors Falls the boat arrived at a stone dock and all the luggage was unloaded. The women sat on the travel chests while the men arranged transport to Chisago Lake. For a lot of money a wagon would carry the luggage, but Anders Peter and his family had to walk the 10 miles on foot. From the dock a narrow road rose steeply and seemingly forever. Glader's wife Elin was exhausted and had to stop several times to catch her breath. The strenuous journey and the loss of two daughters had taken their toll. The road to Chisago Lake was filled with stumps and became increasingly narrow until it was just a path that wound around the marshes and hills.

When the family reached Chisago Lake in the chilly month of October, they were warmly welcomed. Magnus Jonasson had found some

4.2: *Settlements along the St. Croix in Minnesota and Wisconsin.*
   Map: John Linn.

good land and Anders Peter Glader, with the help of his neighbors, built a little log cabin. Just as the friends had planned in Sweden, the two families became neighbors in America.

Back home in Småland, the church had learned that many emigrants suffered great physical and spiritual distress in northern America and planned to start a Swedish Lutheran parish in Chicago. In 1853, the clergyman Erland Carlsson from Älghult accepted the mission. During his three years as a minister in Lessebo bruk, he had become very popular and Bergsrådinnan Karin Aschan[4] was deeply mesmerized by the preaching of this charismatic priest. Her husband Bergsrådet Johan Lorentz Aschan was not amused. Erland Carlsson was active in the revival movement within the state-backed Swedish Lutheran Church and preached that every Christian should live a righteous life and have a personal commitment to his faith. The conservative wing within the clergy of the Diocese of Växjö rejoiced that Carlsson would move to Chicago for the next few years.

When Erland Carlsson arrived in Kalmar at the end of May 1853, he found himself to be the involuntary leader of Kronoberg county's first mass migration to North America. Unbeknownst to him his name had been used in a German travel company's advertisement. Suddenly Carlsson became responsible for the well-being of 176 emigrants. On June 3, 1853, the boat left from Kalmar with the singing of hymns. By way of Germany, the ship reached the port of Liverpool. While sailing across the Atlantic, disease broke out and several passengers died. After arriving in New York, Erland Carlson went on to Chicago where he became director of the Immanuel Assembly. Seventy-eight of the Smålanders who sailed with Erland Carlsson came from Algutsboda and about thirty of them continued on to Chisago County.

In the beginning of February 1854, Östgötlander A. M. Dalhjelm at Chisago Lake wrote a long letter to Pastor Carlsson in Chicago and told him, among other things, that a Swedish Methodist named Agrelius had just held a worship service in Per Berg's barn. Most people hesitated to receive Communion, but Agrelius, once a priest in the Swedish church, said that he adapted the Holy Communion to the audience's beliefs. Anders Peter Glader and his wife Elin were among the few who took communion—despite the advice of more strict Lutherans. Their son Carl did not participate. Afterwards, members who had taken Communion were criticized by old man Dalhjelm who believed that he was now the priest of his own congregation.

Since there was no priest and no church at Chisago Lake in the fall of 1853, some of the Swedes wrote to Erland Carlsson and asked for help. The following spring, he went to Minnesota and on May 13, 1854, the Chisago Lake Evangelical Lutheran Church was formed with teachings founded on the Bible and the Augsburg Confession. Anders Peter Glader, his children and his sister Helena attended this historic meeting in Berg's barn and became charter members. His wife Elin was too weak to attend.

At the first meeting a resolution was passed stating that all teachers and deacons were required to lovingly but earnestly warn and admonish any of the members of the congregation who fell into sinful and wicked ways and to abstain from such discretions as drinking, swearing or gossiping. It was noted that because of the cultural differences in the new country, they should not be too strict to start with.

Despite having no church, the congregation chose to build a school first. It was considered very important that the children received a Swedish education. Glader was elected to the building committee and represented the residents south of Chisago Lake.[5] The committee's mission was to prepare plans for a schoolhouse, calculate how much timber would be needed and decide who would contribute what. When the church was later built, most of the work was performed by the members of the congregation who donated a certain number of unpaid working days. Most had no experience in carpentry so someone needed to monitor the work and ensure that it was done properly. Glader, known as a good supervisor and fine carpenter, was appointed to manage the construction.

Frank Porter knew his uncle Anders Peter well and said he was a man of unusually great strength and stamina. Through the severe trials and tribulations of his life he always remained steady on his feet and looked like nothing fazed him. Anders Peter never revealed anything of what was going on inside—even through the summer of 1854. Still, he worried for his wife Elin's health and about his sister Christina and her family now on their way to Chisago Lake. Glader knew that cholera raged while she was coming to join them and that many emigrants never reached their goal. He asked the Higher Powers to protect his beloved relatives and wished they were already here.

Elin never regained her strength after the trauma and starvation aboard the Franklin King. Over the prior six months she had only walked short distances. At best Glader's wife would go down to the small sheltered bay just north of her house. The sun warmed the sand and sparkled in the crystal clear water. Large leafy trees cast pleasing shadows and the rolling landscape rose up from the shore to a hill. From that high point opposite their log house she could look far over water and forest. Smoke revealed where other settlers built their houses. Early mornings, the silence was broken by the echoing report from a gun. The sound of an ax and the felling of trees carried on the wind. Silhouettes of bald eagles and pelicans appeared against the sky as they fished in the still lake. From this height, Elin could survey her family's new world— but right where she stood this newly arrived immigrant would soon be laid to rest for eternity.[6]

5

About sister Christina's life at Husartorpet, churching, hard times for trained midwives and five compelling reasons to immigrate

As long as Anders Peter could remember, his older sister took care of him. After his mother died when he was only five, Christina was still there. When their father remarried, she continued tending her younger siblings and helping with the household. Eventually 20-year-old Christina started working as a maid at the minister's residence in Furuby until her stepmother Martha again needed help. Christina later worked at Fägerstad Norregård for several years and like other women she longed to have a family of her own; but her father Nils was her guardian and responsible for arranging an appropriate spouse.

Bergsrådet Aschan had confidence in Nils Anderson. So when the nearby farm Husartorpet needed a new tenant, Nils put in a good word for Christina and her seven-year-younger fiancé Johan Håkansson. The young man, the son of a farm owner in Gåtahult in Östra Thorsås parish, was said to be a hard worker. For thirty years Nils handled the Näset farm impeccably and therefore Aschan promised Nils that his prospective son-in-law would be allowed to take over Husartorpet. In April 1830 Johan signed a two-year contract with an option to stay on when the time was up. In return, Johan had to work two days a week at Aschan's farm Truvedsgården in Västorp. During the summer, Christina and Johan also were required to assist with the harvest eight days each.

In late October 1830 Christina's working contract expired and at the age of twenty-nine she was free to marry and move to Husartorpet. On a snowy March day seventy years earlier another twenty-nine-year-old woman had moved to that same place; Christina's grandmother with her husband and a little son. Their old small hussar cottage[1] stood a little distance away—grey, low and now falling apart.

For many years Truvedsgården in Västorp ran a distillery where Johan Håkansson worked at the behest of the distiller. In 1830 they produced 850 gallons of liquor in Västorp and 1900 gallons in Lessebo.

Brännvin, a liquor distilled from wine, was introduced in Sweden in the 14th century by merchants from Lübeck Germany. It was originally used for the production of gunpowder and for medical purposes. As the Swedes learned to distill grain spirits, brandy became available to the common man. During the years of famine at the end of the 17th century there was a grain shortage. Making brännvin for household purposes was banned, but bootleg distilling flourished. Beatings and murder became commonplace and often occurred during a drunken stupor. Brännvin was a central part of social gatherings and in the 18th century it was imbibed daily in mass quantities. Screaming children were shushed using a linen swab soaked in brandy. Booze "cured" hunger, pain and cold. It was both used and abused. Spirits helped people forget about their misery and poverty, but at the same time it brought the very misery and poverty they were trying to escape. In 1809 the ban on making brännvin was eliminated, even for non-farmers, and the taxes were lowered. Drinking became an unrestrained problem. The potato was the most common ingredient for making alcohol and in 1830 over 25 million gallons of brännvin were distilled. At the time, Sweden only had a population of three million. In 1855 to curb the use of brännvin, liquor sales were regulated. Court records show many people, including those in Furuby, were prosecuted and convicted for selling or producing bootleg liquor. In 1860 all private distillation was banned.

After Bergsrådet Aschan joined the temperance movement, these two distilleries were closed and all the equipment sold. In his first winter as a farmer, Johan Håkansson scavenged bog-iron ore from Lake Rottnen to supplement his income. On May 30, 1831 he bought potatoes and a plowshare from Åry bruk. He purchased writing paper too—demonstrating his ability to write.

Shortly after the wedding in 1830, Christina became pregnant. In 1777 King Gustav III decided that all Sweden's midwives had to be trained in childbirth in Stockholm. But the country's farmers could not afford this and the law was quickly abolished. So what help could Christina rely upon in 1831 when she was giving birth to her first child?

In 1830 the main Church in Växjö sent out a notice requesting pastors in Kronoberg county to report if they had trained midwives in their parishes. Only three rural congregations responded positively. Most of the farmers found educated midwives to be both unnecessary and expensive. In the past, women always managed to give birth without them. If things didn't go well, you sent for the provincial doctor in Växjö, something that was very rarely needed.

Most of the priests felt that ordinary women of all ages were quite adept at childbirth, but the church leader Bengt Petrén in Nöbbele regretted that pregnant women still had to rely on "some wives living in the parish, who have not received any other training in Childbirth Science, and have little experience other than from giving birth to their own chidren." From Ingelstad only three wives had died from childbirth in the last 14 years. Two of these had been bedridden before birth. But Hallaryd parish in the southwest part of Kronoberg county differed from most. In that parish 22 women had died in childbirth over the last 20 years, despite the fact that deaths had fallen since they began employing qualified midwives.

When it worked well, local midwives and other women assistants provided continuity and security. The ceremonies and everything else that happened around the children's birth were familiar and created confidence. But it might be the case that the local midwife was an alcoholic and quite unfit or that an untrained woman might try to speed up the birth by urging the mother to push too soon and causing severe tearing of her cervix. In contrast, a trained midwife was able to let childbirth run its natural course and had learned how to turn the fetus in the womb if necessary. Despite her knowledge, the professional midwife was often perceived negatively, a stranger entering the home and immediately forbidding the well-known, ancient rituals. The trained midwives and the untrained local midwives often didn't get along very well. Most times the farmers and their wives chose to use their traditional untrained help. If the birth developed complications then the trained midwife was called for, and by then it was usually too late to save the mother and the child. [Höj95] Was this perhaps what happened in the Hovmantorp/Furuby parishes? In response to the 1830 circular the vicar remarked that there once had been a professional midwife, "but because of some misfortunate events and the poor income derived from her profession, she had to move away in 1824 with her family."

In his five-year report in 1831, Kronoberg county Governor Stellan Mörner noted "the general prejudice against trained midwives and how the reluctance to employ them led to the deaths of many women while

5.1: *Husartorpet in Västorp 1940, just over 100 years after this story.*
Photo: Kerstin Gynnerstedt.

giving birth. Since the state could not afford to pay trained midwives in rural areas, this unfortunate situation remained until the prejudice had been eliminated by continued efforts from all concerned."

Christina first gave birth in 1831. She was tended to by a local midwife and some neighbor women she trusted. After childbirth, women temporarily entered a period of postpartum confinement. They were prohibited from attending church and had to stay at home for four to six weeks. Intercourse was forbidden. In times of poor hygiene this interdiction simultaneously protected the mothers from infections and allowed their abdomen to heal. The mandated period of seclusion also put them at ease, which encouraged breastfeeding. And they were spared from the heaviest tasks—unless poverty forced them back to work prematurely. After the Churching of Women ceremony, which common people looked upon as purification, the new mother was welcomed back into society.

Christina gave birth to seven children in Husartorpet. Her eldest boys came three years apart; Carl Johan 1831, Salomon 1834 and Frans Gustaf 1837. Most often, her sisters from Näset were witnesses at their baptisms.

Every time Christina went to the Churching ceremony, Johan had to pay. Furuby tenant farmers paid 8 shillings while ordinary farmers owed 12 shillings. When entering the church in the 18th century, the woman at this special ceremony had to wait just inside the church gate until a clergyman came and ushered her into the church. Many women felt it was degrading to be waiting down at the entrance like a beggar or a pauper. During the 1800s the mother instead was accompanied by a respected older woman, usually the godmother or some other married female with a good reputation. They passed through the doorway and up to the clergyman. The woman who had given birth to the child fell on her knees and with the words "The Lord accompanies you in truth and in fear for now and forever after. Amen. Go in peace." she was welcomed to the congregation and the social community once again. The priest took the mother's hand and she stood up. Then a bouquet of spices was passed around among the women, all sitting on the left side of the church. Those who could afford it treated everyone with sweets. Sometimes after the service there was a celebration at the church stables where bread, pancakes and brännvin were served. The Church General Assembly banned these festivities, but they continued on anyway.

In autumn 1838 when Christina and Johan had lived on the farm for eight years, Bergsrådet Johan Lorentz Aschan ordered an inspection. The summary document shows that the first floor of the cottage consisted of one room and a kitchen. From the entryway, a staircase led up to the loft, both used as a larder and for storage. It was eighteen years after the house had been built and the front door and kitchen were in poor condition. The stove and baking oven were considered a significant fire danger and the walls needed plastering with a new covering of clay and sand. The kitchen had a dirt floor, which was considered good enough, but the living room floor had to be relayed. Johan had to completely replace the dilapidated barn with a thatched roof. With permission from Bergsrådet Aschan, Johan felled and trimmed many trees, turning them into 72 logs. He also split wooden shakes for roofing. Reusing old timber minimized the cost of the new construction. Previously Johan got permission to construct a root cellar which was still in good condition. The fields consisted of two acres of stone-covered land, which was properly cleared and fertilized. In total, the fields and wetlands yielded about 200 cubic feet of hay, enough to winter four or five cows and three sheep.

In 1839, Johan Håkansson's first daughter was born. The girl was named Anna Maria. She died after three months. Two years later, Christina gave birth to a son named Per Olof and she prayed to the gracious God to give him health and long life. Three months later, the boy died. Another Per Olof was born. When Christina returned to church this time, the son was already dead from cramps. Finally, daughter Helena came into the world and the family was happy to have the little girl. The following year she also died. In the mid 1800s, infant mortality was high and approximately 13% of infants died within 12 months. Two out of five children died before the age of 10, mostly from nutritionally low diets and childhood diseases such as measles, whooping cough, rubella and mumps.

Losing four young children was a tragedy, but in 1850 the death that struck the family at Husartorpet caused the most suffering. Immediately after the confirmation of the second-born son, sixteen-year-old Salomon, died of typhoid. At that time, Christina was 49 years old and too old to get pregnant again.

6

How Christina and her family sailed to North America and about other emigrants on the good ship Cambria

The Cambria was a three-mast ship of 1300 tons (1187metric tons) gross weight. She sailed from Stockholm to New York in the summer of 1854. Aboard the ship leaving from the Swedish capital were tailors, shoemakers, clerks and seamstresses; but also a noble lady's companion [*sällskapsdam*],[1] an editor and a musician. The musician brought his suitcase—and his piano, too! First class passengers included an American hat maker, a Russian professor and three Swedish dressmakers. As the ship sailed south along the coast of Sweden, more farmers, farmhands, tenant farmers, carpenters, soldiers and maids came aboard. Unlike the passengers from Stockholm, the surnames of most of these rural folk ended in "son" or "dotter."

On July 22, 1854 the Cambria arrived at Karlshamn. Glader's sister Christina, her husband Johan Håkansson and their sons Carl and Frans waited on the dock. Beside them sat three travel chests and a bag containing everything they owned for the start of their new life. In a letter from Minnesota, Anders Peter enthusiastically described the new country. He wrote that surely now was the time for the family to come to Ki Chi Saga. He had already located good land on the lake quite close to his own homestead. Son Solomon's death had tipped the balance and Johan and Christina categorically decided to leave this homeland which had stolen five of their seven children from them. Now they wanted to invest in a future in America.

Others from Furuby also would sail with the Cambria. Churchwarden Nils Daniel Andersson from Olsagården had once employed three of Glader's sisters when they were young girls. Now he had sold his farm. He boarded the ship with his wife, six children, nine travel chests, two bags and 17-year-old Elias Pettersson. Their destination was Chisago Lake.

Two teenage boys stood together on the dock, both soldier's sons. They were not burdened by any significant luggage. Johan Artig was 18 years old and the family's future hope. Carl Johan Korsberg was a

57

year younger. In anticipation, he dreamed about the ship that would carry them across the Atlantic. With no hesitation the youngster abandoned his old life as an orphan and a pauper and joyously stepped onto the deck of the sailing ship Cambria. At last he was on his way to be reunited with his big brother who emigrated earlier with A. P. Glader to North America.

In the fall of 1852 Magnus Jonasson wrote his long letter from Chisago Lake addressing it to, among other, his wife's cousin Anders Carlsson[2] living at the farm Tällekullen in Hovmantorp parish. He had no future in Småland, but in North America he could provide for a family and make a future for his anticipated children. He married in March 1853 and the couple planned to spend that summer on Chisago Lake, but he was unable to recoup the money others owed him and their emigration had been delayed.

Anders was a 32-year-old man who planned everything well in advance. So as not to miss the Cambria's departure, he and his wife Ingrid Maria left for Karlshamn at Midsummer. While waiting for the ship he took any odd jobs he could find in the port city. Now Anders and Ingrid Maria would finally proceed west. The Cambria sailed past Skagen and into the North Sea. The first four days were good sailing and the Smålanders expected a pleasant journey. But a storm blew up the following night. All the loose objects on the middeck rolled around making a terrific noise. At the mercy of sea sickness, the emigrants stayed in their bunks. Before the next storm all their possessions were well secured. During the storms Anders never felt seasick, but the pregnant Ingrid Maria was continuously indisposed throughout the entire journey. On September 13, 1854, the Cambria arrived in New York after seven weeks and four days at sea. Captain Perry surrendered the passenger list to the port authorities. A total of 393 people went ashore. The crossing had been unusually successful with no deaths reported and two children born. Anders and Ingrid Maria continued west via train and boat. From New York they journeyed west to Chicago where thieves, swindlers and thugs were waiting for them. While Ingrid Maria sat holding a small child in her arms, a thief grabbed her bag sitting on the floor beside her. Other passengers pursued the thief until he let go of the heavy bag and escaped.

In Rock Island, Anders and Ingrid Maria had to wait a week before they could board the paddleboat that steamed up the Mississippi River. From Stillwater, they took another steamboat to Osceola and then continued on foot to Chisago Lake. In addition to her bag, Ingrid Maria carried a large heavy muzzle-loader gun they bought in Sweden. On the 5th of October, the couple reached Glader's new homestead and were rowed to Lönnö (Maple Island), where cousin Lisa Stina and her family welcomed them. The Linn brothers from Linnehult Södregård lived southwest of Lönnö. Anders knew them well because he had grown up in the nearby small farm Tällekullen and served four years at Linnehult Norregård as a farmhand. When winter came, the Linn brothers went north to work as lumberjacks in the "Big Woods," and while they were gone Anders and Ingrid Maria stayed in Carl Linn's small cabin, together with Carl's fiancé and his youngest sister. Three days before Christmas Eve Ingrid Maria bore a son. Anders took a job at a sawmill 2.5 miles to the west on Green Lake and the following year he purchased a total of 100 acres of land south of Linn Lake.

Glader's sister Christina and her family's long voyage was nearly over and without incident. From Stillwater they steamed on the St. Croix River via the Pioneer, finally reaching Chisago Lake on October 3rd. It was a happy reunion. They had arranged to spend the first winter at Glader's homestead. Elin had become ever weaker and her eldest daughter Anna Maria was now relieved to have her godmother take over responsibility for the household. Anders Peter took the newcomers to the overlook and pointed straight across the lake. A short distance away beyond a sheltered bay the land rose up to a small hill, and here in the leafy deciduous forest Glader found the right place for their new home. To row across took just a few minutes and in winter they could walk across on the ice. After inspecting and approving the land, Johan Håkansson and Glader's neighbor Magnus Jonasson went to the Land Office in Stillwater where the two men registered as much land as they could afford. The price was 1 dollar and 25 cents per acre.

On October 14, 1854, Johan Håkansson bought land on the western shore[3] of the lake, while Magnus Jonasson extended his property to the mainland south of Lönnö. Glader was not in any hurry to pay for his new property, but when they returned from Stillwater, both his brother-in-law and his neighbor Magnus reported crowds of land seekers at the Surveyor's Office. It seemed that half of Sweden wanted to move to Chisago County. On November 10th, Anders Peter went to Stillwater with Carl Linn and payed 80 dollars for 64 acres. Three days after Christina's family arrived at Chisago Lake, Johan Artig from Furuby arrived at Glader's cabin. The boy was heartily greeted by Anders

Peter who helped him get settled. Artig spent the winter in the town of St. Croix in Wisconsin opposite Taylor Falls where he worked as a farmhand for food and shelter. When spring came, Johan worked as a cook for a major road construction project, earning a dollar a day plus food and lodging. Every penny was saved and sent home to his parents. Four years later, Johan's older sister Anna emigrated with her husband Carl Johnson and their half-year-old son. The family left the small farm Ekedahl on Furuby's outskirts and so adopted the name Ekedahl in America. They became settlers on more than 80 acres of land near the shore on Lindström Lake,[4] close to Glader's sister Christina.

Former churchwarden Nils Daniel Andersson from Furuby parish was well off. In June 1854, with great pomp and ceremony, the railway line opened between New York's state capital Albany and Rock Island on the Mississippi River. Nils Daniel rode by train all this way. Arriving at Chisago Lake, the family settled down on the northern shore of the lake and registered 356 acres on which they built their first cottage and a stable from logs. Four years later, Nils Daniel and his eldest son built a large two-storey house similar to their former manor house in Furuby. The new building was named Nya Olsagård. After a hundred years passed, this old house was so full of ghosts that no one dared to sleep there and the property became uninhabited.

The families of Peter and Johannes Pehrsson also sailed on the Cambria. They were brothers and emigrated from Skårtaryd village in Furuby's neighboring parish Dädesjö. Peter settled near Kroon Lake southwest of Glader's new cabin. For shelter from the approaching winter, he dug a traditional Småland hut into the lake bank and for three-and-a-half years, his family lived in this simple home before they were able to build a genuine house. In America, the children took the name Quist. One of the Quist boys married Elin and A. P. Glader's youngest surviving daughter, and the oldest daughter of Peter Pehrsson's married Carl Linn's younger brother.

Johannes Pehrsson settled next to his nephew Carl Linn and the children later adopted the family name Strand. Young Olof Linnell, Magnus Jonasson's oldest son, held Johannes Pehrsson in high esteem. The boy longed for an education but had to work on the home farm and received very little formal schooling. Olof later recalled "My best teacher was an old man who lived half a mile from our place. We called him 'Kyrkovärden' (*the church warden*). Johannes Pehrsson was a well-read man for those days and had what we then called a big library of Swedish books. Johannes was quiet and reserved while in a large group, but if I visited him with just the two of us, then he was very talkative because he knew I wished to acquire knowledge of important matters. I often spent half the night in his company and I always felt welcome." [Lin05]

At Chisago Lake, Glader's brother-in-law Johan Håkansson cleared trees to make room for a house and a barn, but he was killed while felling a tree in March of 1855. Christina lost five of her seven children in Sweden and after twenty-five years of marriage she became a widow soon after arriving to America. Elin became even weaker and Christina was once again Anders Peter's primary support. To earn money in winter, her sons Carl and Frank worked in the great pine forests in the north. Spring and summer the young men cleared trees and brush on the family land, but after two years of hard work, they moved into their first house together with mother Christina. Carl took the surname Lindahl to distinguish himself from all other Johnsons in Chisago County. Though he had just reached the age of 25, it was his mother who was the legal owner of the homestead.

In September 1855 after two decades of marriage Glader became a widower. At first Elin had doubts about the long demanding voyage to North America, but Anders Peter's enthusiasm and determination to emigrate were irresistible powers of nature. During the long nightmare of their journey, she often wished to return to her former calm and safe existence at Berget in Västorp. But at the age of 47, Elin Svensdotter completed her life's journey—from her small hut in Ljuder, to Berget in Västorp and finally to the log cabin at Ki Chi Saga.

Anders Peter hewed her coffin himself and buried his wife on his own land next to the lake. Here where she had stood surveying their new domain, here high and free on this land overlooking the lake, he wanted to be laid to rest one day as well.

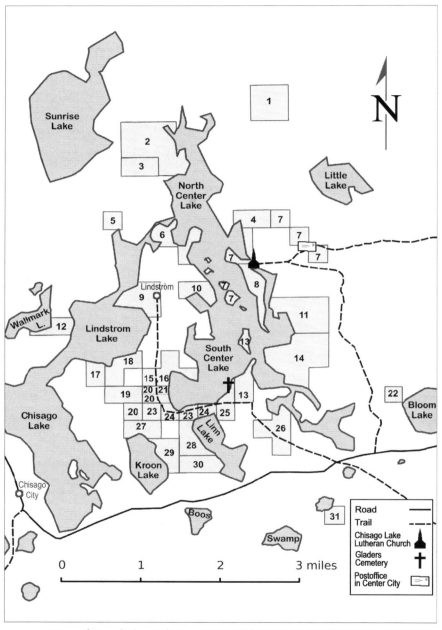

6.1: *Map of Swedish settlers in early Chisago Lake. Map: John Linn.*

6.2: Index of landowners in early Chisago Lake as registered in an early plat map.

Sorted by land Id

Id	Name	Year
1	John Lindgren	1854
2	Nils Daniel Anderson	1854
3	Elias Peterson	1854
4	Jonas Berg	1851
5	Nicolaus Johnson	1853
6	John Smith	1852
7	Anders Swenson	1851
8	Frank Moebeck.	1852
9	Daniel Lindström	1853
10	Anders Peter Anderson Andrews	1852
11	Anders Magnusson Molin	1854
12	Peter John Nilsson	1854
13	Magnus Jonasson	1852
14	Anders Jaenson Porter	1854
15	John Håkansson	1854
16	Charles Lindahl	1854
17	Gustav Johnson Wiberg	1853
18	Carl Johnson Ekedahl	1858
19	Gustav Peterson Moqvist	1854
20	Magnus Peterson	1854
21	Samuel Peterson	1854
22	Gustav Bloom	1853
23	Johannes Peterson	1854
24	Carl Jonasson Linn	1853
25	Anders P Glader	1853
26	Carl Glader	1853
27	Sven Kroon	1854
28	John Jonasson Linn	1853
29	John P Quist	1854
30	Anders Peter Jonasson Linn	1853
31	John P. Johannison Hall	1853

Sorted by surname

Given Name	Surname	Id
Nils Daniel	Anderson	2
Anders Peter Anderson	Andrews	10
Jonas	Berg	4
Gustav	Bloom	22
Carl Johnson	Ekedahl	18
Anders P	Glader	25
Carl	Glader	26
John	Håkansson	15
John P. Johannison	Hall	31
Nicolaus	Johnson	5
Magnus	Jonasson	13
Sven	Kroon	27
Charles	Lindahl	16
John	Lindgren	1
Daniel	Lindström	9
Anders Peter Jonasson	Linn	30
Carl Jonasson	Linn	24
John Jonasson	Linn	28
Frank	Moebeck.	8
Anders Magnusson	Molin	11
Gustav Peterson	Moqvist	19
Peter John	Nilsson	12
Elias	Peterson	3
Johannes	Peterson	23
Magnus	Peterson	20
Samuel	Peterson	21
Anders Jaenson	Porter	14
John P	Quist	29
Anders	Swenson	7
John	Smith	6
Gustav Johnson	Wiberg	17

7

How the party of Smålanders experienced living hell on the bark Laurvig and how life continued on after arrival in the new country

When the wagon left in the summer of 1854, the juror's daughter Katarina Haraldsdotter was inconsolable. For the life of her, she did not want to go to North America. Despite prayers and tears, her husband sold their treasured farm of ¼ mantal at a price of 3,000 Riksdaler Banco. Anders Jaensson decided that his family would be the first to emigrate from the parish, and now he departed with his wife, five children and an aging father. Anders was expectantly looking forward to starting a new life at Chisago Lake with better opportunities for everyone. His wife however felt fear of the future and despair at leaving home. As long as Kataina's house was in sight, her eyes remained constantly fixed on what she loved and knew so well. But her gaze was disrupted. She had to leave the security of home and venture into the scary unknown. Wailing and crying, the neighbors accompanied them all the way to Jät, a distance of 6 miles. In years to come they would tell how terrible this farewell was; they would rather have followed their friends to the grave.

People were emigrating from other parishes too. A party from Östra Thorsås parish joined Anders Jaensson and his family. Several people had emigrated from this parish before and now others followed. The previous year Magnus Carlsson's oldest son and daughter[1] left the farm in Gåtahult, to go to America where they were waiting for the rest of the family to arrive at Chisago Lake. Magnus, his wife and the other six children were heading there too.

In early July 1854, the emigrants departed from Karlshamn. On arrival in Gothenburg, they tried to find a Swedish fast-sailing vessel, but no such ship was scheduled to leave for New York or Boston over the next few weeks. Certainly there would be passage on American ships, but the emigrants were apprehensive about not being able to understand the language while aboard—and the price was too high.

Norwegian ship-owners in Porsgrund and Laurvig 120 miles southwest of Oslo, began sailing emigrants to North America in the 1850s. They could increase their profit margins by building a steerage compartment on top of the cargo, and when these ships arrived at America and the emigrants disembarked, this compartment had to be torn down so the cast iron cargo could be unloaded. Therefore construction of the middle deck had to be easy and cheap. There were no regulations and the space for the passengers was both primitive and inadequate.

The Norwegian bark Laurvig, arrived in Gothenburg with Quebec in Canada as its destination, but Anders Jaensson and his companions had no intention to go there. At the same time, the emigrants were hesitant to stay in Gothenburg for several more weeks as their time and money ran away. After much discussion, the Smålanders decided to sail with the Laurvig. They tried to take comfort in the fact that the tickets for passage cost at least 10 Rd. Banco less per adult than the price demanded by other shipping companies. In addition, the crew was Norwegian so it was easy to communicate with the sailors—and of significant importance was that Captain H. Cock Jenssen seemed to be a "good joe." The bark Laurvig was owned by Iver Falkenberg from Larvik. This would be the ship's first trip with emigrants on board. In a 1908 article from the Nordmansförbundet[2] Captain Cock Jenssen described the trip to Quebec in 1854, and Anders Jaensson also relates the same trip in a letter written October 17, 1854. By combining the captain's and the emigrant's stories, we get a good picture of the conditions on board.

A new deck was constructed on top of the middle-deck beams, with hatches going below to the hold. On this deck, along the side of the ship from stem to stern, the carpenter built two rows of bunks made of rough planks. Captain Cock Jenssen stated that the conditions on board were very primitive and inadequate. He described the aging bark as a miserable old sailor, poorly equipped and leaky. The crew consisted of 12 men. On July 21, 1854 the Swedes boarded while their luggage was stowed on top of the iron bars in the cargo compartment. Most of the passengers were farm-owners or tenant farmers from Småland, but also aboard were a merchant and an official each bringing their families from Stockholm with them. From Gemla manor outside Växiö came Juror Magnus Nilsson with his wife and children. Also leaving Sweden was a Lieutenant who had married for love—but against his family's will because the girl was Jewish. Now the newly-wed couple were emigrating to America.

Everything was ready for departure but the wind was calm. Day after day the sun broiled from a cloudless sky. There was nothing to do except wait for the wind. Six days later at midnight, the pilot got on board and as they passed the lighthouse on the isle of Vinga, he disembarked as the ship set course for the southern Norway coast. Anders Jaensson describes how most of the passengers became light-headed, sick to their stomach and vomited. But the sickness was nothing to worry about, because most of them recovered by morning and felt well again. The Lieutenant and his wife were very happy and cuddled like turtle doves—but when the first really rough seas hit, he too hunched his back, leaned over the railing and vomited. Almost immediately a loud cry was heard: "By all the saints, if I did not lose my teeth!" There was no dentist on board who could supply him with new teeth. From that day on his nose rubbing significantly diminished.

At a stop in Helgera, Captain Jenssen's hometown, about 30 people boarded. They were landlubbers from Drammen inland, and they were not used to the sea. A course was set to the northwest. Three days passed away with good weather and good sailing. Nevertheless Jaensson's eldest daughter Ingrid was not well. The parents became worried and the father went to the captain to explain how her condition was degrading. The captain promised to go to the steerage deck to take a look at the girl. As soon as he saw Ingrid, he said "It's just sea sickness. Do not worry. Tomorrow we will get quieter weather and she will get better immediately." It turned out just as the captain had said. On the next day, their fourth day at sea, the weather was calm and Ingrid immediately began to eat and returned to health. This girl, who for so long had caused her parents so much concern because of her poor health, was feeling better and better every day. Anders Jaensson praised almighty God who now blessed Ingrid and sister Rebecka with better health than they had experienced in the past seven or eight years. The boys Johan and Solomon and little sister Johanna felt good as well.

There were no first or second class cabins on the Laurvig. All passengers paid the same amount, $25 per adult, corresponding to approximately 100 Riksdaler. Captain Jenssen ordered the emigrants to designate two people each day to make sure that the steerage deck was cleaned. Family members lived together in bunks accommodating four to five people. The ship provided straw mattresses but any other bedding had to be brought aboard by the emigrants themselves. The midship location was the most sought after because motion was not as noticeable as it was fore and aft. Apart from the sleeping areas, the space on the middle deck was communal. There were no separate rooms for men and women. The emigrants had to bring sufficient provision for the entire trip across the Atlantic. Mostly they ate porridge, dried meat and bread; the Norwegians brought flatbread and dried lefse, Smålander rye bread and rusk. Tables were provided between the rows of bunks where the emigrants could eat their meals. Every family prepared their own food and shared the same galley kitchen on board located in the deckhouse.

Water was rationed and distributed once a day. Once a week heated water was provided for washing up on deck, if weather permitted. Jaensson's oldest daughter Ingrid turned out to be helpful in cooking and washing for the family. To get on the deck, passengers had to climb up a ladder, which really was a steep staircase. On days with nice weather passengers were allowed to be in the fresh air. Sometimes someone played an accordion and the passengers danced. As with dinner parties at home they also entertained themselves with parlor games and cards. Some of the women wore wooden shoes and homespun wool skirts but this did not prevent them from attending.

Everything went well and the weather was good until the Laurvig arrived a few degrees west of Ireland. Then the storm began. The southeastern wind reached gale force, turned to come about from the northwest, then increased further in intensity and churned up a terrible sea. This pattern was repeated every three days. The storm lasted several weeks and increased occasionally to hurricane force. Under the deck, the emigrants suffered the hell of all hells. Normally daylight reached down to them through the open ship shutters. To keep water out, sailcloth had been stretched over the openings. When it was a rough sea or a storm, the openings were sealed. In the cargo room, the cast iron became rusted creating an oxygen-deficient atmosphere that further worsened breathing for the passengers. Very little light reached below deck from the glass prism skylight in the deck above. In order to avoid the darkness, Captain Jenssen allowed a pair of lamps to burn around the clock on the steerage deck. Day after day, week after week, more than 100 people were trapped in this dark and humid space without any opportunity to get out. The boat pitched and rolled in the rough sea. Suddenly the boat was lifted up and then heavily slammed back down. It felt like the Laurvig could never rise up again but would continue sinking into the depths of the sea. The ship was a living creature that creaked and whined. The rigging was howling and squeaking in the storm. The speed dropped whenever big waves came along and hit the hull with a bang, splitting into a water cascade. When a large wave swept over the deck it found every crevice. Below deck it sounded like the boat had sprung a leak. Passengers feared drowning like trapped rats, while the regular crew furiously pumped the water back out to keep the boat afloat. Many of the emigrants had severe seasickness. They vomited until their stomachs were empty. Then their muscles spasmodically contracted, but only bitter bile and colorless liquid came up. There was not always a bucket at hand. The vomiting ended up on the floor, in their own bunk or on those poor soles underneath them. Finally they lay stunned, completely apathetic, convinced that this was the end. The first dead body on board was Magnus Carlsson's one-year-old son from Gåtahult. The little boy had not had a single healthy day and the parents had been waiting for the pale and sick child's passing since Gothenburg.

During the many days of storms the passengers were forbidden to leave the steerage deck and thus they could not cook in the galley. They became nutritionally deficient and suffered from lack of fresh air and daylight. The emigrants were unable to keep clean or attend to their bodies and their general state of health deteriorated. Cleaning the steerage deck daily as at the start of the voyage was now completely impossible. It was difficult to scrape the bunks clean on the usual once-a-week schedule. The darkness reeked of feces, urine and vomit, and here and there bacteria festered. Many people fell ill with rödsot (*dysentery*) and some died. It began in the starboard's upper aft bunk and spread forward, jumped over to port and continued toward the stern. The first to be affected was a pregnant woman who suffered from both cramps and stroke. A couple of days after the illness started, she gave birth to a child who was tended to by other mothers on board. The baby girl survived but the mother died after three days. As soon as the wind died down, Captain Jenssen, along with councilor Magnus Nilsson, held the funeral. The ceremony was impressive in all its simplicity: Passengers and crew gathered on deck and the sails were furled, the flag lowered to half-mast, prayers were read and the coffin was finally lowered into the sea. Then the sails were raised and the ship was

7.1: *The Norwegian bark Niord of Laurvig was built around 1854. A bark has square sails on the two front masts and a gaff-rigged sail on the mizzenmast. It has a smaller crew than a full square-rigged ship with square sails on all masts. The crew compartment is above deck aft of the foremast. The Norwegian Union "herring salad" flag has the Swedish flag inset in the upper left corner. Photo: Bjorn Eckell.*

under sail again. With this the sorrowful service was over—until the next death. The symptoms of dysentery were a violent diarrhea with an abundant discharge of blood, followed by fatigue. Finally, the victim's entire body became swollen just before death. Strangely, the longer the disease continued, the more the appetite increased until death occurred between the fifth and eighth day. All medicine on board ran out and the emigrants became so desperate that they crushed bricks and baked the powder into pancakes in hopes that this would stop the symptoms. A total of 13 passengers died, mostly children. Among the adults, however, were two men who were heads of families, the "bread winners," who departed their wives and children. More than 50 years later Captain Jenssen relates how the terrible situation onboard the Laurvig, with so many deathly sick people below deck, still rattled his mind. The misery became worse every day. Despite all this misery, these poor, unfortunate people bore their wretched condition with great patience.

Even the crew was infected. When sailor Anders Olsen Bua fell ill and died within a couple of days, the spirit of the crew was broken to its core. Until then, they had been confident that they as sailors would be able to survive in contrast to the poor people who were trapped below deck, unable to get proper food or to keep clean. Now if this hard-working powerhouse Bua had died, could any of them go the same way? The loss of this man, both a good sailor and a friendly person, was mourned by his comrades and by Captain Jenssen. So many of the crew became ill that only a limited number of sails could be manned. This meant that the Laurvig sailed even slower and the journey now took even longer. When the last constipating medications were exhausted, Captain Jenssen became desperate and began to give laxative oil to the sick. Back home he had heard that when nothing else helps, you need to use oil to try to clear the intestines. Nevertheless, he shuddered with the thought of the effect this might have. With the help of God he made good use of the laxative. Every day, the sick improved significantly and no more died.

After three weeks of storm and misery, the weather improved a little. They had now reached Newfoundland's outer banks, but they were threatened by yet another disaster; the emigrants' food was almost totally consumed. Certainly, the ship had some extra supplies but far too little for so many people. Looking ahead Captain Cock Jensen saw that the passengers would begin to die of starvation. His only hope was that the weather would be calm and good so they could catch fish. His prayers were answered and a few days later the Laurvig was to the south of St. Pierres bank. The wind moaned and it became quiet. All the fishing gear on board was used. They were lucky enough to catch four large halibut and 86 unusually large cod. The joy and relief was huge. Now there was plenty of food for everyone on board for the distant future. The wind blew from the west as the ship sailed close to the wind and tacked into the St. Lawrence River heading toward Quebec. Two days later, the captain signaled an outgoing Canadian ship and purchased two barrels of flour. Further upstream he managed to buy more flour and other necessary foods from the Industry, a Norwegian ship from Breivik. With greedy eyes everyone stared at the big slaughtered pig hanging aboard the rigging, but Captain Jenssen was not allowed to buy any of this meat.

Two days later, after a trip from Norway of eleven weeks and three days, the Laurvig approached Grosse Isle[3] outside Quebec. A doctor came to check all on board and six passengers were hospitalized, including some from Anders Jaensson's party. The quarantine quarters had a total of 20 isolation units. Captain Jenssen arranged so that the Swedes lived in the only unit with a large stove. Everyone was deeply grateful to him. In the other units were English, Irish, German and Dutch. Anders Jaensson did not hold the latter in high regard and viewed them as "a barbarian people, rude cowards, crooks, and tramps," by which he meant that none of them looked better than the most impoverished residence of the Täfvelsås poorhouse—and they were murderous, too. Assigning each nationality their own unit was a good idea. Anders Jaensson must have thought so as he often told the story of the time people from three or four countries joined together to fight the Swedes, but turned away before the fight started. There was a store inside the quarantine where the immigrants could buy any kind of food, but it was expensive. Here they sold only wheat bread so thick that it measured at least seven or eight inches.

Just before he left the quarantine, Anders Jaensson wrote a letter home which began:

> Dear brother-in-law and other relatives!
>
> After eleven weeks and five days of sailing on the threatening waves of the Atlantic Ocean we now, praise to the Lord, have reached the long-awaited American harbor and with the joyful announcement that our company, which consists of somewhat more than 70 persons, for the time being is sound and safe, except 3 children who belong to Östra Thorsås parish. Otherwise, on this trip we lost 14 people out of somewhere close to 200 passengers.
>
> Katarina and my father are over the last illness, praise and thank the Lord, who is the helper and doctor of all humans and who has put my beloved ones on the road to improved health. Also I trust in you, my mild and merciful Father, that we all may continue feeling confident. The trip has been slow and difficult because of persistent contrary wind and storms; we have had close to 30 stormy days and nights. We also happened to be on

board a poor sailing ship called Lårvig, but we have had
the advantage of a very decent, good-natured and
capable captain, first mate and their whole crew.

Anders Jaensson states there were almost 200 passengers, of which
about 70 were Smålanders. Captain Cock Jensen recalled 52 years later
that the crew and passengers together amounted to 100 people. The
vessels from the south of Norway, which sailed with emigrants in the
mid 1850s, took from 80 to 150 passengers. By compiling existing data
from different sources it appears that the bark Laurvig had about 100
Swedish and 30 Norwegian emigrants as well as a crew of 14 people
for a total of around 145. Most of the passengers came from Småland,
not Dalarna as mentioned later in the article.

After a short week in quarantine, the Swedes were rounded up by
Captain Jenssen. They were to be taken to Quebec by steamboat. The
farewell hour came a few days later when each one would go on to his
destination. The captain bade farewell to the emigrants. By remaining kind and patient, in spite of all they had suffered, these people had
greatly impressed him. He was deeply moved when he saw the hopeful
smiles in their pale faces. As a memento from this eventful journey, he
received a beautiful forged silver snuff box with the inscription: "Re-
membrance to capt. H: C: J: from the Swedish emigrants, Quebec, 20
October 1854."

The ice had already begun to form on the St. Lawrence River when
Captain Jenssen headed for London in mid-November with a load of
wood. The voyage was beleaguered by tormenting fog and incessant
storms. Much of the time the Laurvig sails were furled to avoid break-
ing the rigging. Large waves washed over the old leaking bark as she
took on more and more water. Day and night they had to keep the
pumps working. The captain did not get home until mid-March 1855
to Helgeraaen in eastern Norway where his future bride waited for
him. Thus ends the article "Emigrant Journeys 50-60 years ago" in the
Nordmandsförbundet in 1908:

> This is briefly what I remember about the memorable
> emigrant trip of 1854. I am now 86 years old, and there
> are hardly any survivors left, but maybe there is still
> someone alive from all these emigrants. Should these
> words reach one of my sorely afflicted friends from 1854,
> then I ask him to receive one warm greeting from an old

man who never will forget how strongly and intimately he became attached to them for the twelve weeks they spent together patiently suffering.

In 1854, the average travel time from the European continent to Quebec was 58 days. The Laurvig crossing had taken 80 days. In that year three emigrant ships headed for Quebec were lost, but fortunately, there were no deaths. One of these ships was crushed after being caught in the pack ice in May. Everyone was evacuated and 145 passengers were standing on the ice with their luggage, until rescued by two other boats. Ten ships arriving in Quebec carried passengers from other ships that wrecked on the way to American ports. Under difficult conditions captains saved many stranded immigrants but had to buy more provisions, sometimes with their own money, just to avoid starvation aboard. If the boat owner failed to reimburse them, the masters suffered a personal loss. Some captains also received sharp reprimands from their shipping companies when they rescued shipwrecked emigrants. Deaths due to illnesses on board increased markedly in 1854. The worst death rate was aboard the English low-fare ships that left Liverpool crowded with German and Swedish emigrants. Also, many immigrants died soon after arriving at Quebec. Orphaned children who no one could take with them were placed in institutions and never heard from again.

Passengers from the Laurvig were advised to stay in Quebec over the winter because of the severe cholera epidemic that had hit America. All immigrants from the Laurvig wanted to continue; the Norwegians to Wisconsin and the Smålanders to Minnesota. During the voyage Anders Jaensson's wife, father and youngest daughter all were sick from vomiting and diarrhea. Now the journey continued on overflowing trains and river steamers. Katharina was infected with cholera and died in Chicago where she was buried by Pastor Erland Carlsson at the Lutheran Immanuel Church. Against her will she left Sweden only to meet death in America.

At Prescott, Wisconsin where the party of Smålanders would begin the final part of the journey, 67-year-old Jaen Aronsson died of cholera. His body was loaded into a box that was quickly nailed shut and rowed ashore. At the banks of the Mississippi a grave was hastily excavated, but no cross or marker was left on the spot. For the rest of his life Anders Jaensson carried the memory that his beloved father did not get a proper funeral and nothing remained to indicate where he rested.

When he arrived in Minnesota, Jaensson visited the land surveyor in Stillwater. Here he bought a homestead at Chisago Lake and received directions to find it. Because everyone was exhausted after the strenuous trip and the weather was turning colder, Anders hired a horse for transportation to Taylors Falls. The family then followed a well-trodden path to the new building on the southern shore of Chisago Lake where Leonard Porter had previously lived. The bachelor had already cleared two of his 57 Acres and erected a small log house before he suddenly died.

Now Anders Jansson needed someone to take care of both the five children and his household. The tenant farmer Petter Nilsson, his wife Lena and their little daughter from Nyatorp in the village of Hörda also sailed on the Laurvig, and now they needed a place to live. The trip had become more prolonged than expected, and it was nearly November. A cold winter in Minnesota was coming. The solution turned out to be for the Nilsson family to move in with the Jaenssons and live there until further notice. In January 1857, Petter Nilsson records the purchase of a new home. That same autumn, Lena gave birth to a son who was baptized "Gustav." He was named after his brother, who had died three years earlier on the long difficult trip on the Laurvig.

There were few women in the Minnesota territory. With so many men, Glader's sisters, Helena and Cathrina could marry anyone they wanted or easily get a job as a servant girl. However Helena probably could not have managed a job as a hardworking maid because of her poor health after the voyage on the Franklin King. As a new immigrant that first winter, Helena Nilsdotter stayed in Stillwater with the family of Christopher Carli, who twelve years earlier had become prominent as the first general practitioner residing in Minnesota. She stayed several

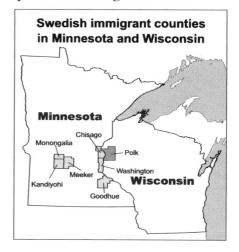

7.2: *Minnesota Swedish immigration counties. Map: John Linn.*

months gaining her strength and doing whatever chores she could manage for the Carli family in return for free room and board.

When spring came, Helena moved closer to Chisago Lake where her relatives and friends lived. Now she worked in the Marine Mills Hotel, 15 miles south of Chisago Lake, and could walk to visit the brother's family and attend worship services. One Sunday she was introduced to a widower with five children. This man was Anders Jaensson and he lived a couple of miles east of Glader's log cabin. In Sweden he had a good reputation. In Helena he saw an unmarried, honest, industrious and godly woman of the right age. She had first been a maid servant at a deacon's home and then for eight years she was a servant for two goldsmiths and a rich merchant in Växjö. In addition, her older brother Anders Peter Glader was one of the leading men in the newly created Swedish community south of Chisago Lake. He was vigorously involved in the planning and construction of both the school house and church. Anders Jaensson from Tävelsås and Helena Nilsdotter from Västorps Näs were married in 1855.

The prosperous juror and farmer Magnus Nilsson, also a passenger aboard the Laurvig, had been praised by Captain Cock Jenssen as "a very good and gracious man who was a great help for me throughout the trip." Magnus came from Gemla manor in Öja parish, just outside Växjö, and arrived with his wife and four children. His destination was Polk County in Wisconsin, located on the St. Croix River opposite Taylor Falls. This area was previously populated by the Dakota people who had been forced out by the Ojibwe tribe. Now the area had about 550 white inhabitants. On the way up the Mississippi River Magnus' six-year-old son Gustaf fell overboard and nearly drowned, "but thanks to merciful God's help, he was saved by two constables onboard the ship." During the financial crisis of 1857 the family lost its small fortune, partly through the dishonesty of other people, resulting in a large debt. After six years of self sacrifice and hard work, the family became debt free. The son Gustaf, at 21 years of age, decided to become a pastor and quickly rose to a prominent position within the Methodist Church In Minnesota. [Alm74]

From Gemla came a young couple who left Sweden to be married. When farmhand Carl Magnus Nilsson worked in the parish he met and fell in love with a farmers daughter Anna Britta Nilsdotter. But they could not be married because Carl was already engaged. Nor could he get a travel certificate. In order to able to be wed, Carl left the parish without permission from the church. He eloped with his sweetheart to be with her brother living in Sand Lake in Polk County.

By 1853 thirty persons had already emigrated from Östra Thorsås. Now others followed to Chisago Lake. Gustaf Johansson from the tenant farm Brunskog visited the pastor in February to obtain a travel certificate to North America. Although the snow was deep and the weather was cold, he now held in his hand the first visible proof that the family's dream would come true. Together with his wife Maria, they would create a better life for themselves and their two children. Unfortunately neither their son Johan nor their daughter Johanna survived disaster on Laurvig. When Maria saw her two children die and lowered into the sea, it was as if life had been taken from her. She became very ill herself, but recovered in the quarantine hospital in Quebec. Together as a couple, Maria began the journey to Minnesota, a journey that sapped the last of her energy. When Gustav finally reached Chisago Lake he arrived alone. Four years later, the widower dared to believe that there was a life even for him. He took the surname "Mellander" and married Anna Stina Samuelsdotter from Attsjö Torsagård in Furuby parish. During the American Civil War Gustav Mellander was one of the many Swedish-born men who sacrificed their lives for their new adopted country.

Hörda Sållaregård in Östra Thorsås too was hit by American fever. Earlier in 1853 two families emigrated from the parish and the single farm-hand Gustav Moqvist, born in Furuby, left for Minnesota as well. Now the newly married couple Carl Gustav Johansson and Lovisa Kjellberg also decided to leave. Thanks to their youth and good health they survived the voyage on the Laurvig and on arrival they bought land near Chisago Lake. In early March 1865 Carl signed up as a drummer in the Minnesota's 4th Infantry Regiment. Shortly after the south surrendered, Chellberg as he was now called, marched far in front of General Sherman's troops in the "Grand Review" victory parade at the capital in Washington, D.C on May 23rd—24th. His wife Lovisa had eight children. Three died of consumption as young adults. [Lea10]

In the early summer of 1854, Ingrid Nilsdotter and her family began the long journey from Hörda Sållaregård to Chisago Lake. Shortly before leaving, she gave birth to a son, but the child died a few days after the baptism. Ingrid, her husband Eric, their two sons and Eric's brother Johan endured a living hell across the Atlantic on the bark Laurvig. From the quarantine outside Quebec, Ingrid sent a greeting to her parents at Backagården in Tävlesås and told them that she and the family felt good. Soon after, both she and her youngest were afflicted with cholera. Only her husband Eric and their six-year-old son Sven arrived at Chisago Lake. Though living at times felt meaningless, life continued. In 1857 Eric Magnusson married Johanna Linn and two years later, his brother Johan married her younger sister Ingrid. The couples eventually settled on farms next to each other in Scandia, but the mailman always confused the brothers and the mail often went to the wrong place. So at last Johan got fed-up and changed his name to Morrison. That solved the problem. [Mor06] Eric and Johanna had seven children. When he died at the age of 58, the youngest son was just eight years old. Ingrid continued running the farm and lived independently until she was 93 years old. Eric's eldest son Sven became a distinguished citizen in Marine on St. Croix. He was, among other things, a shop owner, postmaster and dockmaster for the ferry.

The twenty-year-old farmer's daughter Martha from Gåtahult, was also admitted to the quarantine hospital, but she recovered and ultimately arrived at Chisago Lake with her family. Four years later, she married a well-to-do widower from Östergötland and became Mrs. A. P. Andrews. The couple settled in Lindstrom on what is now called Andrews Avenue. At the age of 42, Anders Peter signed up as a volunteer in Company C in Minnesota's Seventh Regiment and participated in the Civil War for three years. Their son Charles became a successful businessman and sheriff of Chisago County. Their daughter Louise married one of Anders Peter Glader's sons.

In 1796 Anders Johansson died at Fägerstad Röagård in Furuby parish. In the inventory of the estate [bouppteckning] he is referred to as a "danneman," ie. a competent, reliable and respected peasant. At that time, his youngest son Gustav was only one year old. When his mother died 15 years later, the boy left home to start serving as a farm hand in Västorp. At 21 years of age Gustav received the inheritance from his parent's estate,[4] married and bought a small farm in Klintalycke in Hovmantorp parish. Carl Linn's parents moved into the neighboring farm as newlyweds.

In 1830 Gustav Andersson sold his farm and moved to ½ mantal of Gydingsmåla owned by Bergsrådet Aschan. Gustav was looking to advance forward and upward. He wanted to be like his father and was convinced that he was now taking a big step up the social ladder. But after four years of hard work, Gustav's physical and economic resources were consumed. He, his wife and seven children moved to the tenant farm Nyadal.

The elder son Johnannes, just as soon as he had been confirmed, had to go out and work as a farmhand but never stayed long on any farm, always moving on. Twenty-two years old, he married and was admitted as a soldier in Hörda village in Östra Thorsås parish. As a soldier he was given the name Lindgren. Johannes was dissatisfied with his life. He wanted to be a farmer and a danneman just like his grandfather at Röagården. But his father, who had the same goal, was now sitting broken and destitute in a backstuga. Soldier Lindgren became increasingly convinced that his future was in America.

7.3: *Wedding Photo. John Lindgren and Anna Stina Mattisdotter, John's second wife. Photo: Nita Aasen.*

In the summer of 1854 Lindgren left the soldier's cottage under Hörda Norregård in Östra Thorsås, along with wife and four children; twelve, ten, seven and two years old respectively. On July 27, 1854, the family set sail onboard the bark Laurvig. Immediately after arrival in America the wife and two daughters died of cholera.

The surviving half of the family settled in Stillwater in Washington County. There Johannes remarried to Anna Stina Mattisdotter from Vide in Ljuder parish.

In 1862, Lindgren and his wife moved to Chisago County and purchased 160 acres of land near North Center Lake. Twelve years after John had left Sweden with a son and three daughters, he had a new family with one daughter and three sons.

On Friday, February 8, 1901, John Lindgren's oldest son stepped in the Smålandsposten's editorial office in Växjö. The well-dressed man was on his way to visit his childhood hometown Hörda in Östra Thorsås. Mr. J. A. Johnson came to make his success story known in the old country. He did not mention the hardships during the voyage of the Laurvig in 1854, but told how he, as a boy in Stillwater, had to work at a hotel to make money while going to school. After technical studies in Iowa Mr. Johnson moved to Texas to try the livestock industry. When the Civil War broke out, the young man was given this tough choice: either sign up as a volunteer for the Confederate Army—or be hanged. John became a calvary soldier in the Texas Rangers, participated in four battles and was wounded during the assault of Pea Ridge in Arkansas. When his military contract period of one year elapsed, he moved to Indiana and trained to be a locomotive engineer in record time. During the last year of the war, John was employed by the US Government with assignments in Alabama, Georgia and Tennessee. He was discharged with the rank of major.

After the war ended, Mr. Johnson went to St. Louis, Missouri where he married Miss Agnes A. Coler. Due to his diminished health after their stay in the Southwest, they returned north to Marine Mills on the St. Croix River. Here he devoted himself to agriculture and woodworking. John was unanimously elected Sheriff in Washington County six times, all the while studying law.

In 1880, the family moved to Fargo, North Dakota where Mr. Johnson started two successful companies in the agricultural sector. Over the years he held several offices of public trust, was elected as state senator and was a member of the Odd Fellows and the Freemasons. This successful Swedish immigrant was asked to be the American Consul in Gothenburg, with an appointment by the US President, but he declined. For a period in the 1890s, Johnson lived in Caracas, Venezuela and was the CEO of a company in which he was a major partner.

The Swedish American then became the mayor of Fargo for four terms, and won a lawsuit against the railway companies ordering them to return land to the city. The wealth Mr. Johnson acquired through his various companies made possible several long journeys to South America, around the United States and four times to Europe. The visitor also mentioned he was often a foreign correspondent for several major American newspapers.

His trip then continued through Copenhagen and a reception before the Danish Crown Prince. It was clear that soldier Lindgren's son from Hörda had ultimately realized the family's dreams of success and became a well respected man in the new country.

8

About emigrants from Älmeboda and their journey of death in 1854

Samuel Pettersson was born May 19, 1828 on the peaceful farm Deralycke in Linneryd parish in Kronoberg county. If anyone predicted that
many years later this young boy would die far away in a foreign country after being shot at by a band of screaming warriors, they would
have been accused of telling tall tales. Samuel's mother Cathrina Nilsdotter, was a farmer's daughter from Älmeboda and she had married
a 14-year-older widower with four children. On the farm Deralycke in
Linneryd, Cathrina bore a son every two years, and in February 1830
the last one saw the light of the day. At the time the young woman
had been widowed for two months. The estate inventory showed that
the debts were relatively small, but since Cathrina was not able to buy
out the children's share, the farm and possessions were auctioned off.

In Sweden at that time it was forbidden for poor people to move
from one parish to another. A parish meeting was held in Älmeboda
three days after the death of Petter Svensson at Deralycke. It was decided that anyone who brought poor, sick, old or disreputable people
into the congregation would be fined 10 Rd. Then they would either
expel these unwanted people from the congregation or pay their living
expenses. With horror, the 27-year-old widow saw her future life in
Linneryd evaporate. She had no safety net nor means of supporting
her family; poverty waited just around the corner.

Cathrina's preeminent wish was to move back home to Älmeboda
where she had relatives and friends. In 1832 her two brothers Samuel
and Johannes Nilsson rescued their impoverished sister and her children, Gustav age eight, Samuel age four and Peter Johan age two. The
little family moved to a backstuga in Kvesingsbro Södregård in Älmeboda. Before two years passed, the widow married Magnus Nilsson,
a widower, and gave birth to her fifth son; then followed by a daughter and two more sons. But no good fortune smiled on this family,
only poverty and misery stared them right in the face. Cathrina and
the children survived by begging. Her husband was noted as utterly
poor, showed little knowledge in Christian matters during catechetical
meetings and rarely took communion.

In 1836 Samuel and Johannes Nilsson faced a lawsuit in Ingelstad. Älmeboda parish claimed that the brothers were obligated to support Cathrina and her children so that the public would not be bothered by the wandering beggars. Samuel countered that several others in the congregation had also brought in the poor and were not being prosecuted. However he and his brother wanted to do the right thing and therefore agreed to support their sister and Gustav, Samuel and Peter Johan, all born in Linneryd. But they felt they should not have to support Magnus Nilsson's children. In mid-April, the ruling came: Cathrine's brothers were ordered to provide financial support for her and all her children. Church warden Johannes Blom, representing the poverty committee, was pleased. The parish had set an example and also saved a lot of money.

In the catechetical meetings of 1841, Catharina's sons from Linneryd received the highest marks in both reading and Christian study. After his confirmation, Samuel moved in with his namesake, uncle Samuel Nilsson in Binnarebo Södregård. Here the youth had a home and became a carpenter in his own workshop. With the support of his uncles, younger brother Peter Johan went to Lund to learn to be a schoolteacher.

But for Cathrina at the backstuga in Kvesingsbo the situation became even worse. Her daughter had been living in another parish since she was a young child and her ten-year-old youngest son was auctioned off to the lowest bidder,[1] despite the fact that both parents were still living. Was the misery caused by a disease of the body and soul, or by abuse of alcohol?

Magnus Jonasson's long letter about life at the Indian lake Ki Chi Saga arrived in the winter of 1852–53. "America fever" spread rapidly as the residents of Älmeboda repeatedly read over it. The following spring a total of fourteen people from the parish emigrated, but not everyone planning to go to America was able to escape. One of them was the gristmill owner Gustav Collin, who sold all his property and was ready to emigrate—but was hindered by feminine resistance...

Gustav was born in 1806 at Kollebo's soldier's cottage in Älmeboda parish. When his father Nils Eliasson Collin was 17 years old he had been orphaned and subsequently decided to become a soldier in Kollebo. This enabled Nils and his older sister to take care of their younger siblings, saving the parish fund from expenses required to support the very young paupers. Fifteen years later, Nils was finally able to marry, but by then his health had deteriorated and he could no longer do heavy work. That same year son Gustav was born and the family moved to a farm in the village Brunsmåla. Nils Collin's most important interest was not farming but to cure diseases in both people and animals. He studied a Danish book from the 17th century and learned about medicine and other subjects. His knowledge grew and in his notebook he recorded how to cure cows. Due to his ill health, Nils could no longer manage the farm and he began to decline both socially and economically, ultimately ending in a backstuga in Broddamåla.

At age fifteen the eldest son Gustav was sent to Karlskrona to learn to be a carpenter. Five years later the young man was appointed parish carpenter in Ljuder parish. According to his own description, Gustav was so poor that he could not even afford to buy tools, but had to borrow them to begin work. Soon after his father died Gustav moved back home to assume responsibility for his mother and four siblings.

In addition to his work, Gustav collected healing herbs and studied books on medical practices. However, his most inner thoughts revolved around religious issues. Many times Gustav thought the priests preferred to eat well and drink hard rather than help a neighbor in need. He felt sorrow in his heart when he saw the wicked behavior of parishioners and priests. Gustav Collin was not the first in Älmeboda parish to reject the church and instead live by his own interpretation of the words of the Bible.

> The Convention Decree [*Konventikelplakatet*] was introduced in Sweden in 1726 and mandated stiff penalties on laymen who took it upon themselves to interpret the Bible or hold religious services. A fine was imposed for the first offense, but imprisonment or even deportation could be imposed for repeated violations.

Gustav Collin's mother Ingeborg had become accustomed to control and giving orders. She was concerned when she saw the deep religious commitment of her son. His fervor might cause him to neglect his work and tempt him to interpret the words of the Bible and preach them to others. He could find himself in a nightmare and everyone knew what that nightmare was.

"Here a firm hand is needed," reasoned Gustav's mother. She felt the end of her life approaching so she arranged for her son to take a wife. The housekeeper Christina Jaensdotter was selected.

In 1783 Åke Svensson from Älmeboda began gathering neighbors and relatives on his farm in Östergöl. Åke wanted to tell them his interpretation of the words of the Bible. This was the archetype for Christian communities seeking social equality and collective ownership. Initially, the local vicar viewed this favorably. Too many in the parish lived an ungodly life. Those who were devoted and who studied their Bible seeking to live in accordance with the word of Christ could be a good role model. Åke's inner circle included relatives from Älmeboda, Linneryd and Ljuder. Quite rapidly, the movement became radicalized and when the parish priest was not prepared to let the members receive the blood and body of Christ every day, Åke began to hold his own communion services. Marriage to a "non-believer" was considered sinful, while unions between sect members were considered righteous. The Swedish Church condemned this. The bitterness grew on both sides, and the Åkians thought priests were Satan's emissaries. Religious studies and activities began to consume so much time that the farms of the believers became neglected. The Church and State perceived the sect as a threat to the prevailing social order, and the leaders were summoned to the Church Court in Växjö. But Åke's sister Sissa was not intimidated by the clergy: "So dark are ye in your clerical garments, so dark ye are in the eyes of God." She was warned to be obedient and shut up, but instead she replied, "The priests of this earth have a belly full of lard. We hear Satan's servants. Here there are clergymen's gowns and collars, but no priests. The whole world will go to hell—and the priests will go first!" The Church leaders were chagrined and the incident was kicked upstairs to the Göta appeals court and the Royal Majesty. Eventually, the innermost circle of the Åkian's order was declared insane. On January 8, 1786 four men and four women were committed to "Danwik's Madhouse" in Stockholm. There Åke Svensson's 20-year-old step-brother died six months later. After another two years, the 35-year-old branch leader died and so did his stepfather Nils Månsson the following year. Soon afterwards the fourth man was released. The women were kept for eight years. Åke's half sister then married a member of the Danwik staff. Later in life when these women were widowed, they became entitled to special accommodations in the lunatic asylum that was their home for 52 years. Åkianismen, Småland's first revival movement, declined and ceased to exist after their leaders had been detained.

Christina Jaensdotter was a beautiful, intelligent and enterprising woman nine years older than the groom. Her grandfather was Lieutenant Carl Meurling in Älmeboda. At age 80 he fathered a child with Martha, a 25-year-old maid. The old nobleman would never marry the mother, but he continued to live with her and acknowledged Jaen as his son giving the boy the surname Carlsson. Starting at age twelve, Jaen was raised by his half-brother Anders Meurling and wife Sofia Rudebeck at Grisnäs Storegård (now called Grimsnäs) in Ljuder parish. Jaen eventually became a tenant on the estate, but when Anders and Sofia died he left the parish. In the 1820s Jaen returned to Älmeboda with his wife and children to become a tenant at Trällebonäs.

The oldest daughter, Christina, was the caretaker for her parents. When her younger sister married and the newlyweds took over the lease, Christina became redundant. Therefore, at age 35, she agreed to marry Gustav Collin, whose poverty was as great as his devotion. At the wedding in 1832 the couple was given a Bible as a gift from the congregation. With a capable wife in charge, the family managed to save some money. In 1846 Gustav found a suitable investment, a property alongside a flowing stream. After working hard to build a storage pond, roads and a water mill, Källerström's gristmill was finally finished. Eight hundred kronor had been invested.

Gustav and Christina's oldest daughter Anna was cheerful, outgoing, intelligent and outspoken—but was also bossy. Gustav taught her arithmetic and soon Anna became the accountant for the mill. Her sisters Carolina, Johanna and Maria helped run the business and income was good. Suddenly, life changed. Their father Gustav suffered from inflammation of the lung and became bedridden. Then he injured his hand, forcing him to stop working.

For the first time in his life, Gustav completely solidified his religious beliefs. Suddenly the gristmill owner received a divine epiphany about emigrating to northern America where he could freely exercise his faith. But would he be able to leave his safe, structured existence and take his whole family on a dangerous journey? After having received spiritual guidance, Gustav was convinced God's path had been revealed. The faithful believer immediately decided to take the preordained journey and sold the Källerström's gristmill, despite the loud protests from his family. In the spring of 1853 Gustav was ready to go—but his wife and daughters refused to join him. Elder daughter Anna objected the most. She had become indispensable and highly appreciated at the mill. More significantly, Anna was deeply in love with a lieutenant and looked forward to marrying him where she now lived. Gustav delayed his plans and bought the farm Estamåla in Älmeboda.

In the neighboring village of Binnareboda carpenter Samuel Pettersson also planned for a future in America, but had delayed the voyage. His younger brother Peter Johan was studying in Lund and expected to graduate from college in the following summer, planning to return to Älmeboda as a teacher. That winter Samuel drew up plans to emigrate to American with Gustav Collin, even though their motives differed. Samuel's wished to become something more than a poor carpenter in Småland. He would invest in a new life in a country full of opportunities. In Älmeboda there was no future for an enterprising and talented man lacking land or money.

8.1: *Gustav Collin and his wife Christina Jaensdotter. She suffered from a hereditary eye disease and eventually became completely blind. Christina died in April 1863. Photo: Milan Bloom*

Gustav Collin was totally entranced by the idea of journeying to America and could not get it out of his mind. When offered a favorable price for his recently purchased farm, he interpreted this good fortune as the tip of the finger of God. Gustav acted. His daughters realized that this time nothing would stop their father. But when their aunt Catharina said that her family had agreed to accompany them to America, everybody became more at ease. By the end of March 1854, Collin was issued a certificate of travel for his family and his young sister Beata. His brother-in-law Carl Magnus Petersson, a tenant at Trällebonäs, accompanied him to the rectory and received a certificate of travel for himself, his wife and their six children. Both families also received passports for going abroad.

Gustav Collin had previously leased a cottage in Trällebo and was well aquatinted with all the families in the village. Many of them were like him with a deep Christian faith. Early mornings you could hear the farmer at Trällebo Östragård sing while he worked: "Your bright sun rises again. I thank you my God. With power and courage and newborn hope I am singing the sounds of joy." When the church bells tolled Saturday evenings, both he and his wife stopped whatever they were doing to silently read the Lord's Prayer. The old grandmother on the same farm performed her own evening ritual, unfazed by the boisterous children. When she began to untie her apron and read Psalm 440: "My clothes are taken off. Bury my sin, oh God, Bury my sin, oh God..." it became strangely still around her. While singing she undressed to her smock, said her evening prayer and went to sleep. [Lag62]

In Trällebo Bosgård, homeowner Jonas Johansson wanted to emigrate in 1853, but with a wife and six children he thought it was too risky. His elder son Nikolaus had gone on ahead to America to better understand what the arduous journey would be like. He wrote back encouraging letters from Chisago Lake. At age 52, Jonas Johansson sold his farm in Trällebo and emigrated with his wife Caisa Ergilsdotter and their five youngest children. Son Johannes and daughter Christina each of whom were married, accompanied their own families as well.

In April, carpenter Samuel Pettersson went to the parsonage to get a travel certificate. He had finally decided to emigrate to Chisago but did not have to go alone. Ultimately a total of forty people from Älmeboda and several from Linneryd and Dädesjö left in 1854.

On May 12 of that year, the ship Woodbury of New Orleans arrived at Gothenburg to take on passengers. All of the 450 emigrants were Swedes. Gustav Collin seems to have taken the role of leader for one of the groups of emigrants from Älmeboda. On the passenger list, the ship's officer entered Collin and his family, then Carl Magnus' family followed by Samuel Pettersson and Sara Israelsdotter with her little girls. Also the Johansson family from Trällebo sailed with the Woodbury. On board, the normally strong and happy Anna Collin completely changed. Her father Gustav had offered her a family allowance and permission to stay in Sweden and marry. Whether the daughter's beloved lieutenant got cold feet or if Anna chose to leave him and join her family we do not know. Her good qualities were described as intelligent and outspoken, but she was considered nervous and vulnerable, too. It was said she lost her will to live and was very ill when the boat arrived at Boston on July 22, 1854. The family continued on to Chicago where Anna died of cholera. Her family gathered beside her deathbed. For those present her death was very emotional and traumatic. Anna claimed her father destroyed her life and she openly expressed her hostility toward him. Only in her old age would her sister Johanna speak about this terrible experience. When she did, tears streamed down her cheeks and her hands trembled...

Pastor Erland Carlsson quickly buried another Swedish immigrant in the cemetery at the Immanuel Church in Chicago. The Smålanders who brought the infection with them were urged to leave the city as soon as possible. Despondent, they continued their voyage up the Mississippi River—along with their constant companion, cholera. Gustaf Collin was a medical expert and ordered his family to remain isolated, avoid food served on the boat, boil all water and refrain from swimming in the river. According to family history, his younger sister Beata disregarded his suggestions. She took a swim, fell ill, died and was subsequently buried on the sandy riverbank. When the Swedes arrived at St. Croix on July 31 they were taken to a small island named Lamars. The authorities were afraid the cholera would spread and so the immigrants were quarantined. In his autobiography Gustav Collin said many of his friends lost their lives there.

At that same time Gustav Blom visited St. Croix. He also was born in Älmeboda parish, but moved away with his family to Linneryd when he was ten years old. The long-standing bachelor belonged to the inner circle of people emigrating with Pastor Erland Carlsson in 1853. Gustav was a true Christian and always devoted the day of rest to reading the Bible. He embraced the thought of the Pietists[2] and lived in trust of God. It was his Christian duty to do good deeds every day. Blom had registered 60 acres of fertile land in Chisago County on the small lake that now bears his name, Bloom Lake. Instead of spending his efforts building a house, he devoted his waking hours to clearing the forest and slept in a simple shelter at night. When the Smålander took a job as a day-laborer in St. Croix, he was told about the newly arrived Swedes in quarantine. Blom took what money he had in his pocket, bought food, borrowed a boat and rowed out to the island. The first person Gustav saw was Carolina Collin walking down to the shore from a cottage. The 31-year-old bachelor fell headlong in love. This was the woman he wanted to marry. A week later, the Collin family was permitted to leave their quarantine and two days later they were staying with friends in Chisago. This story was recorded in the *Bloom and Collin Family History* written by Milan Bloom. The depiction of the first meeting between Gustav and Carolina was a romantic juxtaposition to the story of tragedy and many deaths.

Almost fifty years later, Nikolaus Jonasson from Trellebo disclosed what happened to the family at the end of the long journey in 1854. In St. Paul Jonas Johansson and family stepped aboard a steamer and headed to Taylors Falls. The trip from Sweden to America had taken sixteen weeks. Everyone survived the strenuous journey and were glad to be near their long-awaited goal. When the boat passed the city of Hastings in Minnesota, the father began feeling weak. It became eminently clear that he, his son Elias, his married daughter Christina and her little child all suffered from cholera. All four died that same afternoon. The captain ordered the bodies to be taken ashore immediately, but promised to wait until the next day before he buried them.

It was only a few miles to Osceola in Wisconsin, and an envoy was sent to fetch Nikolaus Jonasson from Chisago Lake. The surviving family members dug four shallow graves on a small island in the St. Croix River. The site was well marked, but winter was on its way. Half a year later an unusually strong spring flood swept away all traces and marks. The graves were never found.

Cholera was known and feared even in Småland. In the unusually hot summer of 1834, the first epidemic came to Sweden, taking more than 12,000 lives. Hardest hit were Gothenburg, Stockholm and Jönköping where $\frac{1}{5}$ of the population died. Unlike several other epidemics that killed many children, cholera claimed victims of all ages. The disease could be shockingly fast; one who fell ill in the morning might die that evening. The infection spread through contaminated water and the cholera bacteria thrived in bad sanitary conditions.

Many of the afflicted had little resistance. The incubation period was usually two to three days, but watery diarrhea sometimes appeared after just five hours. Fluid loss could be five gallons a day and quickly led to dehydration and death if no remedy was taken. In the 1850s, doctors did not know how cholera could be prevented or treated.

Those who emigrated in 1853 wrote home about the good news of their arrival and told their relatives and friends to follow. But this year the letters told mostly of illness and death. The cholera epidemic that broke out in North America in 1854 hit all the new arrivals especially hard because their health had already been diminished after the exhausting sea voyage. During the land journey to Minnesota the immigrants were crammed onto trains and aboard crowded riverboats where the sanitary conditions were very poor.

In 1854 the newspaper Korsbaneret (*Banner with Cross*) published an article about a large group of immigrants from Linneryd and Älmeboda. It said many were infected with cholera and died on their way to Chisago Lake. The steamboat captain did not want to bring these contagious immigrants to Taylors Falls so he left them on the river bank several miles south. They found neither people nor houses there, just a miserable hut formerly used by lumberjacks. Several of the Swedes who died were simply buried without coffins in the sandy riverbank. Only sticks and hands were used to dig the graves. After a couple of days, relatives and friends at Chisago Lake heard the horrible news and came to rescue the survivors. The newspaper said the Americans burned all their luggage to prevent the spread of infection. When the surviving Swedes finally left that place, coyotes dug the corpses out of the sand and ate them.

9

How Samuel Pettersson found his mother's namesake, about Glader the builder and how the Swedes survived the financial crisis

A huge triangular-shaped forest of tall pine trees called the Big Wood lay between the St. Croix and Mississippi rivers. The US Government acquired the land in 1837 through a treaty, including a clause recognizing the Indian's right to hunt, fish and harvest wild rice and maple syrup. Even when the area belonged to the natives, the white man trespassed and cut down thousands of trees. Every winter loggers invaded the Big Woods and millions of logs were harvested and hauled away to the frozen rivers.

When spring came, the logs were dumped in the St. Croix River and driven downstream to water-powered sawmills. One of the first mills was established in 1839 at Marine Mills, later called Marine on St. Croix, located about 15 miles south of Chisago Lake. Vast quantities of trees were sawn into lumber and both the industry and the city grew rapidly. The millworkers lived in large barracks at night and worked in the mill by day, sawing logs into planks; a risky job where lack of attention had catastrophic consequences. Marine Mills incorporated the sawmill, some residential houses and a hotel. Sisters Helena and Cathrina Nilsdotter from Näset worked in the village. They wished to live as near to their siblings at Chisago Lake as possible.

Many of the Swedes who immigrated in 1854 lost close relatives in the cholera epidemic and sought solace in their remaining family. Samuel Pettersson from Älmeboda survived the nightmarish voyage, yet all his friends and relatives were still in Småland. During the day he cast his recurring visions of horror aside, but at night he was constantly awakened by deeply disturbing dreams. When his visions tormented him at their worst during the "hour of the wolf,"[1] he was confronted by death and despair.

Soon after Samuel arrived in Minnesota, he met an unmarried Smålander with the same name as his mother, Cathrina Nilsdotter. Women were scarce in the frontier and Glader's youngest sister already had many marriage proposals, but she was not inclined to accept any of them. Here in America the 28-year-old immigrant could be selective and wait patiently for the husband she really desired.

In the summer of 1855, Samuel and Cathrina discovered they were to be parents. The young couple wanted to get married and join the Swedish Lutheran Church in Center City. Church rules demanded potential members have recommendations, which Anders Peter Glader and Gustaf Collin provided enthusiastically.

When Joris Pelle Andersson emigrated from Hassela in 1850, the 17-year-old farmer's son Erik Norelius followed him to America to study for the ministry. Four years later, Norelius's whole family arrived to settle in Minnesota whereupon Erik guided them to Chisago Lake. The newly established church-in-the-wilderness had not yet succeeded in finding a Swedish Lutheran clergyman. Most priests in Sweden were not attracted by this opportunity "to go beyond where the road ends" to lead the spiritual instruction of poor Swedish settlers, so Erik was convinced to stay and teach the children. A small meetinghouse was hurriedly constructed in Center City and in summer 1854 the prospective priest started holding school and worship services. This did not go completely complication free.

The congregation had several differing views on how a sermon should be structured and Håkan Svedberg, the most orthodox member, discounted Norelius' ability. In addition, both Baptist and Methodist pastors tried to proselytize members to their own worship services. At home as a young man in Hälsingland, Erik learned "Don't think that you are better than anybody else!" [*en ann e´ så go som en ann*]. Treating other villagers as inferior was just not how one acted. Now that Erik began to lead the worship too, he had a problem. On the weekdays he was a brother; just another member of the congregation. However, on the Sabbath he was expected to be the leader and father figure to guide the members in living their lives. In his memoirs, Norelius described a chance encounter that led to the solution of his conundrum. One day, the young theology student went for a walk. He was plainly dressed in an old pair of overalls and strolling with a walking stick in one hand when he met Gustav Collin, a much older man. Collin removed his hat and bowed deeply. During their conversation, Norelius discovered that Collin held him in high regard, with great admiration and piety. Erik looked searchingly at Collin seeing only conviction in his innocent blue eyes. This affirming experience spurred young Norelius to embrace his role as the congregation's priest. In September, he left for Chisago to continue his study for the priesthood.

The following summer, Norelius visited his family at Chisago Lake. Now the small room in the schoolhouse could not hold everybody during religious services since the congregation had grown so large. Half of the audience had to stand outside to hear the word of God. Later in *Hemlandet*, the first Swedish-language newspaper in America, Erik described how awful the singing of the psalms sounded. He sang the way it was written in Dillner's[3] Psalm book. However, the lead singer standing beside Norelius sang in another tune, maybe according to a hymnbook of which Eric was unaware. An old woman near the door sang the loudest of anyone and led the other little old grannies in song. A man on the other side of the door sang loudly too, leading the rest of the men. Those standing outside sang even different melodies. Norelius stated "a very strange-sounding music; like music never heard before even in the liveliest beehive." However, such cacophonous singing

In the old Swedish church, the words "melody" and "harmony" did not belong in the same sentence. Even the cantor sometimes had difficulty getting it right. The singing of hymns was influenced by the local tradition of secular music; one slid into the notes, warbled the "frills" and sang in the local dialect. A single hymn could have several different melodies and the common folk preferred singing loudly rather than in tune. Around 1820–30 the Swedish Church decided that the hymns should be standardized. The slower German variant with a note on each syllable became the norm. In the 1830s the psalmodikon was introduced, a simple string instrument that you could build yourself. From the pulpit, the audience was urged to go home, make their own psalmodikon, and practice the hymns with the correct melody in the new slow way. More church organs were purchased and trained cantors hired. But when hymns were not sung in the time-honored way, it brought bad blood:

> Shut up you pathetic sacristan dung!
> Who the devil asked **you** to come?
> We've been here since we were young.
> We damn well know how hymns are sung!

Magnus Gustafsson, *Music in the South*   [GG86][2] of hymns was the norm at many other Swedish-American churches. If only every good singer would teach the others, they would surely enjoy an inspiring and edifying rendition of the hymns in church.

Erik Norelius' article in *Hemlandet* in 1855 stirred up such strong reactions that the editor received many angry letters from Chisago County. Because of the strong language, these letters weren't published.

In the spring of 1855, Swede Peter Cederstam accepted the challenge to become the congregation's new priest. In July when the first Sunday school was organized, Gustav Collin from Älmeboda became one of the teachers. At last this profoundly religious man could devote himself to his long-held dream inspired in Sweden; to interpret and preach the Word in the Bible. After completing religious instruction of fourteen young people, Pastor Cederstam celebrated the first congregational confirmation ceremony on August 19, 1855. Among the participants were Anna Maria Glader and two neighbors: Lena, Carl Linn's younger sister and Olof Linnell, Magnus Jonasson's oldest son.

Pastor Cederstam soon noticed how difficult it was to lead these wayward Swedes of Chisago Lake. All the members of the congregation wanted to build a church, but no one could agree where it would be located. The Swedish farmers were accustomed to consensus decisions within their village and though they quarreled with each other, they always stood united against the world outside. Now the men refused to give in to a bunch of strangers in order to reach consensus. In early July 1855 two carpenters from Älmeboda, Gustav Collin and Samuel Pettersson, were chosen to decide how much lumber they needed. Then some strong-willed member of the congregation fought to build the church as close as possible to his own home. Anders Peter Glader and early pioneer Per Berg offered to donate part of their property if the church were to be built on it. Both had ambitions and wanted to create a community with God's temple and themselves at the center—ensuring both wealth and immortality.

When Erik Norelius first talked about the Swedes at Chisago Lake, he claimed forest dwellers have livelier and tougher dispositions than those living in the plains. He noted the settlers were resilient, straightforward, stubborn, and sometimes trenchant—especially at the parish meetings, a situation Norelius experienced himself firsthand. The different groups began arguing that the church should be built near their own settlement. Then the men scolded each other until some were so angry they immediately stormed out and went home. This same pattern was repeated at the next meeting. Norelius said the Swedes around Chisago Lake were molded by the wild wilderness where they lived. That wouldn't be an issue as long as they didn't forget the ten commandments—which he feared some had already done.

Years later Pastor Cederstam elucidated how he managed to break the deadlock over the location of the church. The different factions had agreed to build a church in Center City—as long as retired soldier Moebeck donated a two-acre plot—knowing full well he had no intention to do so. Suddenly inspiration struck. Cederstam decided to make a $50 offer to purchase the land. He scraped money together by gathering all the cash he had on hand and borrowing the rest from a kitty reserved for a newspaper subscription. Then Cederstam visited Moebeck's home to discuss the difficult situation at the church and laid the money on the table: "I have come to buy some land. Look! Here is $50 in gold and silver. Mr Moebeck, please take this money as payment for two acres of land for the church. Tomorrow you can go to the Land Office in Stillwater and buy forty more acres of land next to you." But Moebeck didn't really think the congregation was serious about buying his land. "It's me buying the land and I'm the one to loose it if this doesn't succeed," countered the pastor. Finally, Moebeck agreed and shook his hand.

After the service the following Sunday Cederstam announced that the congregation could now own two acres of Moebeck's land—something to which everyone agreed.

"But how much will it cost?" wondered the Smålanders. "The land has been bought and paid for and will be handed over to the assembly when you agree on the plan," said Cederstam. "I bought the land and paid for it myself. But you all know I am poor and I have only done this so we could all agree. If anyone were to contribute fifty cents, or just twenty-five cents, it would be welcomed."

Within a couple of weeks, the congregation had donated 60 dollars to purchase the land. In September 1855 the congregation elected a building committee to represent the various factions. Anders Peter Glader was elected chairman a few days after his wife's funeral.

Two summers earlier, young Erik Norelius served as a teacher and pastor at Chisago Lake. In 1856, he became a priest and wanted to start a collaboration between all the newly-formed Lutheran parishes in Minnesota. A meeting was scheduled in Center City. Norelius and

9.1: *Anders Peter Glader was chosen head of construction when the first church-building was built. Its dimensions were* $45 \times 30 \times 16$ *feet. It took less than a year to build. The tower was built later.*
Photo: John Linn. Original: Church archives.

his colleague planned to go by a steamboat departing from Red Wing in the afternoon of October 4, 1856, but the steamboat was late and they had to wait until three o'clock for its arrival the next morning. At sunrise the priests landed in Prescott, Wisconsin. There they took the stagecoach to Hudson and walked to Stillwater where they stayed the night. The next day the young men walked thirty miles on foot in the pouring rain. When they neared Scandia they met a Swedish family who gave them shelter for the night. The following day, the priests rode behind an oxen team to Glader's new cabin at the southern part of Chisago Lake where they were rowed across the lake to the church.

Norelius arrived at noon on October 7, a full day late. While the meeting was going on, mass was held every afternoon. Sunday worship service included Holy Communion and people came from far and wide to attend.

The framing for the church in Center City went quickly, but now it stood as an empty shell without an interior. Benches were just loose planks and a simple desk served as the pulpit. In November 1856, Anders Peter Glader from Furuby and Gustaf Collin and John Elmqvist from Älmeboda were chosen to propose how much and what kind of timber was needed to build the interior. The congregation also wanted a fence around the church, but times were tough and cash was a rare commodity. Ultimately, it took several years to finish the church.

The Lutheran Assembly of Center City was overseen by the minister, three deacons and three trustees. The deacons were responsible for social matters including rule enforcement and charity. The trustees were responsible for secular financial matters. The assembly enforced strict rules. Members absent from the worship service for three months or negligent of their children's Christian education were first given a warning. If there was no improvement, then they were ostracized. Dancing was considered a sin. Members of the parish caught dancing at the Midsummer celebration at Chisago Lake had to sign a letter asking forgiveness and agree to distance themselves from such deplorable events in the future. If anyone refused to write a letter of apology, they were not allowed to take the Lord's Holy Communion until they confessed their sins to the church council.

Even back home in Sweden, the antipathy toward dancing and fiddle playing intensified in the 1850s. Priests in the burgeoning Free Church and also in the religious revival movement within the Church of Sweden were opposed to such worldly pleasures. According to an uncorroborated story from the Konga district, the following event occurred sometime after the mid 1850s. Prosten[4] Andersson in Hovmantorp had a farm hand who liked to dance. One evening when the priest and the farmhand were driving past a house where many young people were dancing and their unbounded ebullience was in full swing, the priest told the farmhand to get out of the carriage and peer through the window. The boy did as he was told and inside he saw many evil spirits walking around the dance floor, whipping pairs of dancers whenever they did not dance fast enough. After that, he never went to participate in any get-together where people danced.

In 1856 devastating land speculation ran rampant in Minnesota. New towns were staked out and given names. People expected quick money by buying land, and then selling it for a large profit. Blind greed spread. Land prices rose to unreasonable levels, all financed with loans at high interest rates. In 1857, the bubble burst and North America suffered an economic crisis. Banks failed and their patrons lost their money.

Hans Mattson lived south of Chisago in the Swedish settlement of Vasa in Goodhue County. His parents in Önnestad in northeastern Skåne had been affluent enough to send their son to school. He studied mathematics, Christianity, geography, history and foreign languages including Latin, German, Greek and French—but not English. Hans joined the military; but as a farmer son he had little chance of a successful military career. In the spring of 1851 18-year-old Hans Mattsson and his friend Euström left Sweden seeking a better life on the other side of the Atlantic.

During their first year in America, the new immigrants suffered severe starvation, illness and frostbite. The youths were not used to hard manual labor, they had no profession nor trade skills and their book-learning education was of no use since neither of them could speak English. Their situation improved only after Mattson's father and brother arrived the following year.[5]

A few years later, Hans Mattson lived with his wife and child on a small farm at Vasa, Minnesota. After selling the farm for a good profit the family moved to the flourishing city of Red Wing where he became a merchant. Sales were good and Hans did well. Captivated by his early success, the Swede continued to speculate and invested his newfound wealth in city lots in prospective new towns that existed only on the paper. Mattson, his friend Hans Euström and their families moved to Geneva, which they expected to grow to become a big city and multiply the value of their land.

Now in the summer of 1857 the economic crisis struck. Minnesota's financial infrastructure crashed. Ninety percent of the so-called paper towns were never built—including Geneva. That autumn Hans Mattson moved in with his in-laws. After a personal audit, he found himself without any real estate and with $2000 of debt at a 5% monthly interest[6] Mattsson had to sell everything he and his wife owned, including housekeeping supplies, furniture and even his wife's gold watch.

In Chisago County, the Swedes had been denied credit purchases from merchants or loans from banks. Instead, they lived a Spartan life based on self-reliance. Many Yankees referred to them with disdain as "The Wooden-Shoe People," people who wore wooden clogs on their feet [*träskofolket*] rather than leather shoes. "Better wood on the feet than in the head," the Swedes would say. They were now secure in their new homes and watched while many Yankees lost everything and had to return to the east.

In the fall of 1855, Glader's 29-year-old sister Cathrina married Samuel Pettersson and in February 1856, their daughter Mathilda was born. When the economic depression struck, Samuel could no longer support his family as a carpenter. In mid-October 1857 he bought 28 acres of land from Carl Linn's cousin Magnus Pettersson from Dädesjö and his wife Ingrid. Now, Anders Peter Glader and the sisters Christina, Helena and Cathrina owned new homes on the southern shore of former Indian lake Ki Chi Saga. The four siblings lived close to each other once again, but now on another continent.

10

About life and death in the old country

Two patriarchs of Hovmantorp and Furuby died in 1856, Johan Lorentz Aschan in Lessebo Bruk and Nils Andersson at the farm Näset, both 83 years old. They were energetic and demanding men but with widely different ranks on the social ladder. The farm Truvedsgård in Västorp linked them together. Over 45 years, Bergsrådet Aschan owned Truvedsgård, while Nils Andersson was his tenant. Through hard work and with the help of children, wives, and hired hands Nils at Näset under Truvedsgård created an unusually high standard of living for an ordinary tenant farmer. At Nils' death the estate inventory showed a surplus of 256 kronor. This was a small sum compared to a farmer with full ownership, but a good financial statement for the 83-year-old tenant farmer nevertheless. At J. L. Aschan's death, the bergsrådet's fortune was estimated to be approximately 3 million kronor.

> Johan Lorentz Aschan first became a well-known physician and surgeon in Småland. But his real calling was as a powerful industrialist tycoon. He purchased the iron works and paper mill in Lessebo and made them highly profitable through innovation—and through ruthless exploitation of the local inhabitants. He was given the honor and title Bergsråd, a senior executive for the Bergskollegium, a government bureau in charge of conducting and controlling mining and metallurgy operations. It was an extension of the rule of the King. Thus he exerted a great amount of overt political and economic control over the Smålanders.

Early on the day of Nils' funeral on June 6, 1856, everyone gathered in the house of mourning. Both adults and children walked up to the casket for the viewing and afterward the grown-ups were treated to aqua vitae and snacks. After the coffin was sealed, a highly respected man in the community gave the eulogy while standing on a pile of firewood so that all could see and hear. The ceremony at Näset in Västorp ended with a hymn. In the Furuby congregation, strong voices

10.1: *Funeral guests gather at the house of mourning to bid farewell to the dead. The ground around the coffin is strewn with cut spruce boughs. The small evergreen spruce with the broken crowns symbolize the end of life. Photo: A. C. Hultberg in the early 20th century. Östergötland museum.*

were much more appreciated than good singing—and it sounded like it. When Sweden became Christian in the 1100s, the dead were no longer buried at home but in the cemetery instead. Roads did not extend to most farms so the corpse had to be carried to the church by pallbearers. Lanterns or torches lighted the way on dark early mornings. The men were sorely taxed by the heavy coffins as they trudged down narrow paths and rutty roads or over the ice-covered countryside and deep snow. Early in the morning the men chosen to carry the coffin were given food and liquor, more than sufficient to dull the pain. When they were properly anesthetized with brandy, long poles were attached to the sides of the coffin, sticking out beyond so that men at each end could lift the polls onto their shoulders and march off with their heavy burden.

Before the procession started, the brandy flask and a piece of crusty bread were passed around and among the pallbearers who tipped their hats in the name of Jesus. It was important for a funeral procession to be noticed as it passed by. The more the ruckus the better. The participants made lots of noise for the first few miles, but eventually their strength began to wane. When the procession finally arrived at the church, pallbearers and mourners alike were completely exhausted. Over the centuries roads improved, but the custom of hoisting the casket and carrying it to the final resting place endured. A story from the early 1800s tells of an old woman who demanded of her children: "With so much I have acquired and left to you, you can at least afford to have some virile pallbearers carry my coffin to the grave rather than just throwing me on a cart like an old beggar woman." [Sto72]

In Västorp, it had always been the crofter's task to carry the corpse to the cemetery, but by the mid-1850s this old custom would soon disappear. Nils Andersson had long lost count of those he himself had carried to their last place of rest. Surely he would want the same courtesy: to be carried on strong shoulders to Furuby church. However, Nils' probate record included 12 shillings for transporting a casket, so the coffin probably was carried to the church by horse and wagon. To honor the dead, spruce boughs were cut and arranged in patterns and displayed in front of each farm and cottage along the route. In Furuby, the clergyman and the keeper of the vestments met the procession in front of the church and preceded the coffin to the cemetery. The deceased was lowered into the grave and the priest spoke the traditional words "From earth thou art. To earth thou shalt returneth." A number of shovels had been placed around the burial pit. While the closing hymn was sung and the bells pealed, the men filled in the grave. When they were finished everybody left the cemetery and returned back to the house of mourning.

Funerals were important events that reflected the reputation of both the family and the deceased. The death celebration at Näset cottage provided plenty of food and brandy. A total of 12 Rd. of Nils Andersson's estate were spent on his funeral, about one third the value of a cow. The money was paid for: the coffin, digging the grave, the conveyance of the casket and the funeral refreshments—and the usual religious indulgences of money for the poor, the priest's fee and a small gift to the church.

Only four of Nils' ten children attended the reading of the estate inventory on June 16, 1856. Daughter Britta Catharina, or Cajsa as she was usually called, was the oldest at age 64. She began working as a maid at age ten and later was forced to marry a man more than twice her age. Her husband recently died and Cajsa was officially a widow and now could manage her own affairs. Two of her four children had reached adulthood so she lived with her married son in Södra Sandsjö. Cajsa was known to be a quarrelsome woman and the relationship with her daughter-in-law was very strained. At the baptism of each of her son's children, he was the one who presented the baby, a very rare and perhaps a stopgap measure. The priest even noted Cajsa's bad temper in the church registration book where he urged her to be more compliant.

Nils Daniel, Nils Andersson's 52-year-old son was also present at the reading. He worked as a farm bailiff[1] at Aschan's farm in Lessebo. There he met his future wife who bore him six children. After six years, Daniel tried to be a tenant farmer at Äng in Västorp, but the grass was not as green there as he had hoped. A few years later, Daniel returned to Aschan and worked as foreman of the farm Högaskog. At the death of his father no one expected he himself would die four years later.

Lisa, the daughter from Nils' second wife married soldier Anders Danielsson Ståhl from soldier cottage 36 in Furuby. Lisa was 40 and had given birth to six children. Married women were not considered "of age" at that time and therefore Lisa was only recorded as "Soldier Ståhl's wife."

Youngest son Johannes now ran Näset, taking over the tenant contract. He was 37 years old and married to Maria from Röagården in Fägerstad. They had four children and a fifth was on the way. He had a talent for working with animals and was known for his well-behaved oxen. They were only disciplined with words and gestures and were never struck or harmed. Johannes was kinder to animals than to humans. Nils' son bore a heavy burden; he had to cover the rent to Truvedsgården with four or five days work a week, tend to the cottage, take care of his parents and pay the hired hands.

Also, Johannes had to provide for his own growing family. Earlier, when his father Nils ran the farm, the older children worked at home without compensation and the family was relatively prosperous. But now in the 1850s the croft could no longer afford horses. Two old saddles and some bridals were all that remained of Näsets' former glory.

Johannes too wished he could leave for Minnesota, but as the youngest son he was destined to take care of the farm and his aging parents.

Six people were also eligible to inherit from the estate, but were not present. Son Anders Peter and Nils' three daughters were in America. Daughter Christina had become a widow while Helena and Cathrina were each married. Son Jonas' daughters Maria and Anna grew up on the farm at Nyäng and were now adults with their own families living in Hovmantorp parish. These absent heirs shares were managed by Nils Håkansson at Berget.

Nils Håkansson too had hoped to go adventuring with Anders Peter Glader, but Nils' wife Lisa Stina would not risk her family to the dangerous trip to America. But Death decided to claim her husband at the farm Berget, not in America. Nils Håkansson attended the funeral at Näset, but two months after the inventory he died suddenly at age 30 from stomach inflammation. It is said that one hot summer's day Nils laid down and took a drink from the brook. He died a few days later on August 16.

10.2: *Lisa Stina Johannesdotter (1821–1908).*
Photo: Kerstin Gynnerstedt.

10.3: *Erik at Berget. Berget and the well-kept farm in Västorp was still in the family in 2017, owned by Lisa Stina's grandson Erick Johansson. Note the low ceilings. Photo: Ingvar Malmberg.*

Nils Håkansson left four underage children between the ages of two and eight years old. His cousin Daniel Jonasson, a juror in Tollstorp and the brother of Magnus Jonasson living at Chisago Lake, was appointed their guardian. The law of 1743 required the inventory to be registered at the district court. The inheritance documents were preserved, so we can follow what happened after Nils Håkansson's death: The reading of the inventory was held on November 24, 1856. In case there was no debt and some excess money, the widow was entitled to withdraw 5% as the survivors share before the rest of the estate was distributed.

Reported assets		Reported Liabilities	
The property Berget	1500 Rd.	Loans, bills, expenses	1138 Rd.
The inventory	543 Rd.	Nils was custodian for the	668 Rd.
Outstanding supplies	592 Rd.	children at croft Ängsmon.	
Total:	2636 Rd.	Total:	1806 Rd.

The surplus was 830 Rd. and Lisa Stina chose to take a cow, a heifer calf, a pig, a featherbed and a wall clock as her widow's share—in total valued at just over 50 Rd. The remaining assets were split in half as evenly as possible, each half categorized by: copper, tin, iron, wood products, agricultural implements, other bedding, deceased's clothing, cattle and miscellaneous. The widow was arbitrarily assigned one of the two halves and the children shared the other. The debts were divided in a similar way.

An announcement from the Furuby church pulpit broadcast news of the auction to be held at Berget in Västorp on March 6, 1857. Buyers would have three months after the auction to pay for their purchases. The bidders purchased about 150 item-groups. The items of the children's share, valued at 228 Rd., actually sold for 614 Rd. at auction. The widow wanted to keep most of the items on her list, but to do so she must bid like anybody else. She paid 145 Rd. in total. The best ox at Berget cost Lisa Stina 83 Rd. but with this purchase she could retain her entire trained oxen team. However, the horse sold for 33 Rd., a price the widow could not afford. Nor could she keep the dresser, her pride and joy, that sold for 22 Rd. Her indispensable loom and accessories sold for twice the estimated price. Lisa Stina was able to buy back her beds, food cabinets, tables, milk pails, shovels, a large Swedish ax, a spit, a frying pan, pots and an iron cooking tripod. She also indulged herself by bidding on the serving dish from her porcelain china set, a few coffee cups, two glasses, a tin stoup, various books and a book of sermons. [Kro33]

Auctions were very popular and well attended at that time. Everyone at the auction was enthusiastic and in high spirits—except for the seller liquidating the estate. Auctions were one of the most appreciated community get-togethers and usually they were augmented with liquor and fistfights. For several years afterwards Nils Håkansson's clothes were seen on other men, but it was Lisa Stina who bought her husband's hat. Later when Frans Gustaf came of age, his mother gave him his father's hat, a manly symbol of maturity.

Nils Håkansson never went to America, but his wallet did—Carl from Ekedal bought it and then emigrated to Chisago Lake.

The year after Nils Håkansson died, his younger brother Johan Olof worked as a hired man at Berget. We can only speculate whether he had hopes to marry the widow and thus take over the farm. As a widow, Lisa Stina Johannesdotter was independent, but if she ever married she would become a dependent again. Also, she was only 35 years old and might become pregnant at least five more times.

But Lisa Stina was now in charge of her own destiny and she chose to run the farm herself with the help of a hired man and her four children, just as her great-grandmother Giärtrud had done at Gydingsmåla more than 100 years earlier.

11

About Jonas Peter Falk, whose grave Vilhelm Moberg stood in front of and contemplated what caused such an old man to emigrate

When Vilhelm Moberg visited Glader cemetery in 1948, he stood quietly in front of Jonas Peter Falk's tombstone. Here was a person born in 1793, well before he came to America. For a long time, the author pondered why this old man uprooted his way of life in Sweden to invest in a new life so far away from home. When he emigrated Falk must have been well past his prime, yet willing to face the difficulties of acclimating to a new country.

In 1861 at age 68 Jonas Peter Falk arrived in Chisago County along with his two underage daughters. According to family history, the previous winter he and his girls lived in a root cellar in Tollstorp, a small community in Småland's Hovmantorp parish. What had brought this unfortunate man to that humiliating fate?

Jonas Peter Falk was born September 17th, 1793. At the early age of thirteen he started working outside the home, but returned after a year to help his mother Helena take care of the croft and his little sisters. Between 1810 and 1815 the boy worked as a farmhand.

> Jonas Falk's father Peter Pehrsson Falk served in the Kalmar Regiment and lived in soldier's cottage No. 70 in Hassla, Lenhovda parish. [Kal] During King Gustav the Third's Russian War 1788-1790 Falk served on warships and participated in several naval battles: at the southern coast of the Swedish island Öland on July 26th 1789, at Reval[1] on May 13, 1790, in the battle of Viborg bay on July 3rd that same year and at Svensksund[2] a few days later. Because of the Pomeranian war 1805-1807, the Russian War 1808-1809, the Napoleonic War 1813-1814 and the Norwegian War 1814, soldier Falk was often away from home during the years 1805-1817. [Hog]

In this part of Småland, forestry and agriculture were very important aspects of people's livelihood. Most of Hassla's men mastered the art of building charcoal kilns. In 1795 eight farmers from the small village produced and sold 240 loads (17,000 ft³) of charcoal to Klaverström forge. By doing so they earned more than 130 Rd., equivalent to the price of eleven cows.

Toward the end of September 1817 Jonas Peter Falk moved to Hovmantorp parish to work for the industrialist Bergsrådet Johan Lorentz Aschan. First he worked as a farmhand on the Fetebo farm and subsequently became a crofter at Ekåsen under the farm Lillagård. Now Jonas was able to support a family and he married Anna Maria Andersdotter from the croft Glasholmen in Tollstorp. On January 22ⁿᵈ, 1820 daughter Lisa Stina was born and in the spring of 1822 they were blessed with a son Anders Peter.

Anna Maria's brother and sister-in-law were fairly well off. They tried for several years to have children but could not. Now they wanted to be the foster parents of Lisa Stina, a fact registered in the clerical census. But mother Anna Maria could not give up her little daughter so Lisa Stina stayed with her biological family most of the time.

Falk had to pay 39 Rd. tax to Lessebo each year to grow crops and feed one or two cows on the Ekåsen croft. The fee was paid by working two man-days per week at the Fetebo or Lessebo farms. Residing in the cottage cost Jonas Peter and Anna-Maria each eight additional workdays per year, half of these days during harvest time.

As a crofter (*tenant farmer*) under Aschan, Falk was obligated to make charcoal, a skill he learned growing up in Lenhovda. He made each delivery to Lessebo bruk furnace and every one was recorded on a square tally stick including the year, supplier number, name, place of residence and whether Falk produced it, transported it or both. After the reckoning at the end of the season, he got to keep the lower part of the stick which was a receipt for the number of deliveries. In the most productive year he delivered 1200 ft³. Falk also earned extra wages by cutting timber. With the help of an ax he hewed tree trunks into square beams, the equivalent of 72 man-days of effort. He also chopped 300 sheaves of aspen leaves as feed for Lessebo's horses, and both he and his wife performed extra day-work.

Bergsrådet Aschan was very pleased with the industrious couple at Ekåsen and offered Jonas Petter Falk use of ¼ of Gydingsmåla. The whole property could support 12 cows, 4 heifers, 12 young cattle, 3 horses and 24 sheep. If Falk excelled Aschan promised that the family could live the rest of their lives on one of the finest farms in the parish.

The law required that any ironworks must have access to sufficient charcoal before launching or expanding a business. Charcoal production required large forested areas. Farmers within a
7-mile radius of the iron works were obliged to manufacture and
deliver charcoal. Periodically during the 18th century when the
price was too low, the peasants refused to manufacture charcoal. Thus to insure an uninterrupted supply Aschan bought
many farms around his iron works—the closer and the more
forested the land, the better. To get the most out of each property strict work contracts were signed with tenants, foremen,
farmhands, maids and crofters.

Full of belief in the future Jonas Peter Falk arrived in Lessebo on
January 29th, 1824 to sign a contract with Johan Lorentz Aschan. Falk
and a married farm-hand named Johan Persson each leased ¼ mantal
of Gydingsmåla. Falk was to pay for his share with two days work
every week in return and Johan's lease was the same. Wintertime days
lasted from 4 AM to 8 PM, but in summertime they had to work as
long as it was daylight. In addition each wife was to work 24 days
every year, half these days at harvest time. The tenants agreed to attend
to the buildings, fields, meadows and forest and keep them in good
condition. They also were to maintain part of the road between Växjö
and Ingelstad and a half-mile of road on the property, which at the
time was in good condition. The forest provided pine, fir and birch for
use as timber, firewood and fencing materials. Every year the tenants
were required to produce charcoal from the forest to sell to Lessebo
bruk at a fixed price. Furthermore Falk agreed to transport goods six
times a year to Kalmar and Karlskrona anytime Aschan requested. To
advance from being just a poor crofter on Ekåsen to a full tenant of ¼
Gydingsmåla, Jonas Peter had to make some investments. At the end of
February in 1824 he borrowed 50 Rd. cash at 6% interest from Lessebo
bruk.

Anders Peter Glader's grandfather Nils Thorsson was born at Gydingsmåla in September 1725. Since boyhood he worked diligently aim-
ing to take over the farm one day, but his dream was never realized
and at age 29 Nils left in anger. Over many years his twice-widowed
mother Giärtrud had managed the farm, fully determined that Gydingsmåla would continue to follow tradition and pass the farm down

through the female side of the family. She arranged a marriage between her daughter and a man twice her age. He had money to invest in the farm and agreed to continue the female succession. June 9th 1753 the girl turned 15, the legal age to be wed, and two days later she married. This was the greatest day in Giärtruds life. Nils was devastated and moved to Västorp.

The married couple operated the farm successfully and eventually passed it on to their youngest daughter Catharina. Sixteen years old she married the respected farmer Gustav Johanesson. He bought the neighboring farm and now the family owned the entire estate of Gydingsmåla. Gustav was an ambitious farmer and a respected member of the local mining council.

In 1812 the family suffered two fatal blows. First the son, age 10 died of whooping cough. Then Catharina's husband Gustav died of tuberculosis at age 44. The estate inventory recorded Gydingsmåla as a rich farm with inventory worth 1190 Rd. The silver alone was estimated at 122 Rd., including nine silver cups, three of them gilded. The entire estate included the whole of Gydingsmåla as well as one of the farms of Fägerstad Röagård. The two farms also owned 200 Rd. of grain held in the Furuby and Hovmantorp parish granaries and several other outstanding assets. When the liabilities were included, the net worth was 1444 Rd. The widow inherited half. [Joh60]

Now 35-year-old Maria Catharina was obliged to take care of her elderly mother and three minor children. She could choose to run Gydingsmåla by herself as her grandmother Giertrud had done or remarry, but no longer be in control. What she needed was a good farmer who could both invest in the farm and successfully operate it. Giertrud married Olof Nordström. That was not a wise thing to do...

In 1806 Olof Nordström was employed at Lessebo bruk as a masmästare, the highest ranked profession in an ironwork. He was responsible for the production of iron. Blast furnaces at that time were charcoal-fired and had to be torn down and rebuilt about every 25 weeks. Nordström also supervised filling the blast furnace with iron ore, flux and charcoal and the processing of pig iron. He earned 1 Rd. a day when filling the blast furnace and 2 Rd. a day while working round-the-clock smelting pig iron. In 1817 Nordström was promoted to senior supervisor, the oldest and most skilled masmästare in the region.

Catharina's first husband Gustav had operated Gydingsmåla with the help of several paid farmhands. He made a good profit farming the fields and forests. But Nordstrom began running into financial difficulties as both a furnace supervisor and a farmer. He bought goods on account and borrowed beyond what he earned in salary. In addition, he took loans at 6% interest from the Aschan company. In 1820, he and his wife were forced to sell the farm Fägerstad Röagård. At Gydingsmåla the buildings and fences deteriorated. The fields, meadows and pastures were neglected. Catharina's children left home after their confirmation; the sons moved from the parish to be farmhands and the daughter married young. Only her son and Olof's son Johan remained on the farm.

In 1822 the family's financial situation was poor and Olof Nordström needed money, so on December 28th Johan Lorentz Aschan eagerly loaned him 1000 Rd. at 6% interest and with 3 months notice. Only 58 days later, Aschan called in the loan. Nordström failed to pay the debt. The next day Aschan wrote a request for enforcement of the loan. In addition to the debt and interest, he demanded payment for expenses too. Olof Nordström found no way out of this pickle. On November 10, 1823, he sold Gydingsmåla to Aschan for 3000 Rd. Olof and Catharina were entitled to use half of the estate at a rate of 4% of the purchase price per year, and for this they were obligated to maintain the houses, fields and meadows as well as pastures and forests.

On the 25th of March 1824 Johan Lorentz Aschan achieved his goal with ownership over another heavily forested farm located less than a mile from Lessebo bruk. He took over the estate Gydingsmåla, and that very same day Jonas Peter Falk arrived with his family.

Jonas and Johan Persson were to jointly manage half of the property and also share the housing. The main dwelling was big, 50 feet long and 35 feet wide, and it had two living rooms on the ground floor. Falk's family would live in the west half and Persson the east. In the middle there was a communal kitchen and vestibule, and a shared room in the attic.

The house was in need of repair. The roof was leaking and had to be re-thatched with birch bark and the walls had started rotting and needed new wall-boards. In Falk's living room the wall paneling had to be replaced and whitewashed, the ceiling needed repairs as did the baking oven and the chimney in the kitchen. The vestibule required a new door.

The largest of the outbuildings Jonas Peter and his wife used was just over 55 feet long and contained a stable, feed storage and a barn. The walls showed signs of rot and some parts needed new boards. This work was estimated at 11 working days. The shingle roof was dilapidated and 250 new shingles at 4 sh. per shingle had to be put on top of the old ones. Also the ceiling in the sheep shed had to be repaired.

Jonas Peter kept his cows in the second barn while Johan Persson used the stable. A door was missing and the roof was dilapidated, as was the ceiling of the cowshed. Further Falk was responsible for repairing and maintaining a grain storehouse and completely rebuilding the barn where the marsh hay was stored. The tenants were required to fix the registered deficiencies in return for 16 shillings per workday.

Falk and Persson shared ten acres of farmland yielding a modest rate of return. But the fields contained many large stones partially buried in the ground and a lot of rock cairns. Within the next six months they had to remove six of the largest rocks and add them to a stone fence. Jonas Peter was obligated to cut brush from his land, which took 13 days. All three tenants of Gydingsmåla shared the pastures, but clearing them had long been neglected. It took a total of 60 days work to remedy the situation. Falk's share was ¼ which meant another 15 days of tiring labor. [Gyd30]

Two days a week he had to work at Aschan's farms in Fetebo or Lessebo, three and five miles from Gydingsmåla. From April to October his working hours were from sunrise to sunset and Aschan's crops had the highest priority. When the weather was good for harvesting, the tenant farmers could be ordered to work additional days, at times resulting in their own hay or rye or barley being ruined.

In 1824 his wife Anna Maria had two little children and was pregnant, but nevertheless performed her 12 long day's work during the harvest at Fetebo. On November 3rd, a daughter Sara Helena was born.

In February 1825 Jonas started repairing the house. This winter he only performed 7½ man-days work for Aschan, but instead produced and transported 31 loads of charcoal to the kilns at Lessebo bruk, which was a more lucrative proposition. Bergsrådet promised Jonas Peter that during the first year he did not have to make the six transport trips to Kalmar and Karlskrona as part of his annual tax. But this was not recognized by the bookkeeper who incorrectly increased the tenant's debt by 25 Rd., the equivalent of 75 winter workdays. Soldier Falk had taught his son to read and write with beautiful penmanship and also to count. Jonas Peter had bought writing papers and kept an account of what he owed and what work he had done. The bookkeeper's mistake was obvious and Lessebo bruk paid him 25 Rd. to compensate for the incorrect billing.

In order to transport cargo as required by his contract, Falk bought two young oxen on credit from Fetebo farm in February 1826. This increased his debt by an additional 75 Rd. On March 13th, Jonas Peter began his first transport to Karlskrona. At a speed of two miles an hour, each trip to Karlskrona and back took about a week. The first outbound load consisted of plowshares and for the return load Falk carried roofing tiles and salt. To get decent pay the load should weigh 1½ skeppspund³ or about 560 pounds. Thus the first trip was a light load and paid poorly even though it took a week.

On April 12th he picked up a heavier load of iron and nails for Kalmar. Five days later he received a return load of pig iron. Now the loads were metal and the trip went to the harbor using seaport standards by which it only took 500 pounds to get paid in full. On June 12th, Falk carried a load of paper to Kalmar and received pig iron for the return trip over a period of eight days. On July 1st, he felt content with a job well done and bought snuff and a hymnbook for 28 shillings each—a total cost equivalent to 3½ days wages.

The trip to Karlskrona at the end of July turned out to be a bad deal since Jonas Peter had to drive home without a return load. Six days later it was time to haul iron and nails to Karlskrona again. This time he brought back a barrel of herring and a box of 800 bottle corks. The trip took a week and did not pay more than what he would have earned working just four days. On September 30th, he hauled a load from the Lessebo paper mill to Kalmar. The return load consisted of limestone and soap. In October Falk drove herring to the Klavre mine and hauled quicklime back. For six days, he also carried bog-iron ore to Lessebo bruk. This year Jonas Peter spent a total of five weeks hauling long distance freight.

When the harvest failed at Gydingsmåla, Jonas Peter and his wife. Anna Maria knew that their food and the animals forage would not last to the next harvest. They dreaded the impending starvation. Anna Maria could only perform nine days work while caring for three little children, so Jonas Peter worked seven extra days with his oxen to pay what she owed. This year he performed all his own work requirements and as payment for producing and transporting 13 loads of charcoal to the blast furnace in Lessebo bruk, Falk received 19 Rd. Nevertheless, his debt to Lessebo bruk increased. It was now 82 Rd.

On January 14, 1827 bad weather hit. The snow was falling and the wind was blowing. During the night the snow stopped and the wind died down. Early the following morning Jonas Peter drove to Lessebo bruk to pick up a load iron rods and begin his journey to Kalmar. In the evening the wind started blowing from the north, the temperature fell and by next morning it was below zero. During the following two days it was sunny and calm but it was still very cold sitting on the sleigh. Jonas Peter tried keeping warm by walking next to his horse, but it didn't help much.

On the morning of January 18th it started snowing again and Falk was happy to arrive at Kalmar later that day. He picked up a cargo of three barrels of grain for the return trip, but both Jonas Peter and the horse were exhausted and needed to recover before making the arduous drive home. After a couple of days the cold front passed, the temperature rose and the wind started blowing from the east. The snow was now mixed with rain. Both Falk and his horse struggled against the wind and through the slush. Wet, frozen and completely exhausted he arrived back at Lessebo. This task had been painfully long, life threatening and exhausting—for both himself and his valuable horse. Though Falk incurred unanticipated expenses along the way, he was only paid 2 Rd. for this shipment.

> 1826 was a remarkable year of high temperatures and dry weather. It was one of the two worst droughts in that century; only the drought of 1868 was as bad. In places no rain fell between sowing and harvesting. Still today the month of May 1826 remains the driest on record in Sweden and September 3rd 1826 the warmest day of that month. Due to the dry and hot weather large forest fires raged throughout Småland and many other provinces of Sweden, causing significant damage. The air was filled with an unpleasant sticky smoke and men gathered from miles around to fight the fires. The grain crops were a disaster and the hay harvest was less than half of what it normally was.

This was the first and only cargo he hauled to the ports in 1827. Over the coming years Jonas Peter rarely traveled such a long distance, and only when there was no risk of snowy or cold weather. Hauling freight in winter over long distances was too great a risk. The tenant realized he was better off producing charcoal than suffering on the roads, so the remainder of that year Falk earned a total of 45 Rd. delivering charcoal to Lessebo bruk.

Falk's harvest in 1826 had been very poor. To avoid famine in the spring of 1827 they even ate their seed corn. In May Jonas Peter bought two barrels of barley, which they used to sow the fields and to make porridge. This cost him 32 Rd., corresponding to 96 days of labor. In those days, rye bread was a staple. You could survive for a long time on it. In July Anna Maria's grain became depleted and she could no longer bake their daily bread. To stave off starvation, Jonas Peter bought rye on credit in Lessebo for 13 Rd. and 16 sh. Anna Maria could not leave their three small children home alone to go to work, so Falk and his oxen worked 6 extra days on Aschan's farms to satisfy half of his wife's unfulfilled day works. Although Anna Maria's husband performed all his work requirements that year their debt to Lessebo bruk continued to increase.

In June 1828 Jonas Peter hauled liquor to Kleva and brought a load of foundry equipment back. That same month the family grain ran out again and he had to buy 2½ more bushels of grain, corresponding to 18 work-days. This year Jonas Peter made only two trips to the harbor towns and instead delivered charcoal to the blast furnace. He performed all his day-work and Anna Maria assisted for ten days at the farms in Fetebo and Lessebo during harvest. The eight, six and four-year-old children had to stay at home by themselves.

In 1829 the debt to Aschan was up to 117 Rd. Falk performed all his day-labor tasks. He produced and delivered charcoal to Lessebo bruk, thus compensating for the insufficient work hauling goods. Even with all that, his situation became untenable. The longer Falk worked for Bergsrådet Aschan the more his debt grew. By 1826 Johan Persson and his wife had given up and his successor Israel Pettersson lasted only two years. Being a tenant on ¼ Gydingsmåla did not turn out to be the financial boost that the families expected.

Despite all their efforts Jonas Peter and Anna Maria's financial position degraded so badly they were forced to sell most of their valuable possessions to Johan Ludvig Aschan. On April 25th, 1829 in the presence of two witnesses, Jonas Peter Falk signed a purchase agreement at Lessebo:

1	redish-brown horse, 14 years old	20	Rd.
1	heifer red backed 1¼ year old	16	Rd., 32sh.
1	steer, ½ years old	5	Rd.
3	sheep 3 Rd. each	9	Rd.
1	wagon, needing repair of rear wheels	5	Rd.
1	cabinet, painted brown	3	Rd.
1	chest for clothes, brown	5	Rd.
1	wall alarm clock without clock house	6	Rd.
1	copper kettle with iron feet	5	Rd.
1	copper kettle	3	Rd.
1	iron pliers	2	Rd.
2	items—charcoal 13 loads + 14 loads	4	Rd.
	Total	93	Rd., 32sh.

After the sale the cattle remained in his care until further notice, but now was considered company-owned livestock and had to be carefully tended. Bergsrådet bought the painted chest Jonas Peter and Anna Maria used to store important documents as well as clothes, textiles and a book of the gospel. That chest was precious. It was the only piece of furniture a farm hand or a maid owned from the day they left home. It was a small portable personal space that followed them from farm to farm every time they moved. The belongings stored inside had been acquired at the expense of much hard work and were associated with their future dreams. Aschan also bought the expensive wall alarm clock, a symbol showing Falk had advanced from crofter to becoming a tenant at a big farm.

The family made every effort to create a future at Gydingsmåla. While living on the little farm Ekåsen, Anna Maria became pregnant every two years, but during these last four years no child had been born. It was impossible to reconcile the periodic birth of children with the many compulsory tasks of tenant farmers. Now their sacrifice seemed meaningless and another life was once more growing inside Anna Maria.

Falk's contract was canceled but he had to wait until March 25th, 1830 to move out. To pay all his debts to Aschan, the animals and the carpentry and farming tools were sold at auction on November 20, 1829. Former parliamentarian Magnus Jonsson from Ormeshagahult was the auctioneer and sold the items for a net sum of 170 Rd. When the debts were paid, 42 Rd. remained. On January 24, 1830 daughter Lena Cajsa, was born. Two months later the family left Gydingsmåla.

At the end of August 1830, the fences at Gydingsmåla were assessed. To be considered a good fence the wood polls had to be four feet high and a mediocre one at least 2 feet high. Less than that, the fence was deemed worthless. All mediocre fences were a liability to the owner and assessed at one shilling per fathom and unacceptable fences at two shillings per fathom. The result of the surveyor's calculations showed that Jonas Falk had kept his own fences relatively well. The majority were in good condition. Only 150 feet of fence was unacceptable, resulting in a debt of almost 8 Rd. But more than half of the 6.5 miles of fencing at Gydingsmåla had been jointly managed by the three tenants. Thus Falk was charged for ¼ of the total debt owed and had to pay another 18 Rd.

Earlier in that year Magnus Jonsson from Ormeshagahult surveyed Gydingsmåla and as a result Falk had to pay 43 Rd. for the deficiencies. Thus for the total time he was a tenant he came up 1 Rd. short. In addition, Jonas Peter and Anna Maria previously sold their most valuable personal possessions to J. L. Aschan. After six hard years as a tenant, the family left Gydingsmåla on March 25th, 1830 poorer than when they arrived.

On that very same day, Olof Nordström's family also left Gydingsmåla where his wife Catharina's ancestors had lived and farmed since the 17th century. The family was succeeded by Gustaf Andersson who once owned a little farm in Klintalycke, but was enticed by the ambition to become a tenant of one of the finest farms in the parish ... Five years later his economical and physical assets were gone. Gustav moved to a croft with his wife and their seven children. A few years later he was living in a hut. His eldest son became a soldier and was assigned the soldier's name Lindgren. In 1854 he sailed with his family to North America aboard the bark Laurvig.

Falk's successor at Gydingsmåla was Samuel Israelsson, formerly self-employed but forced by debt to leave his farm. After a few years as a tenant, Samuel was demoted to a farmhand and his wife had to work under the "white whip." She milked the cows early every morning—again in the evening—every day—the whole year.

On March 25th, 1830 Jonas Peter and family moved to the soldier cottage at Tollstorp Norregård as a tenant. Merely a few acres of land belonged to the soldier's croft but Jonas Peter was an industrious man of several skills. For many years he constructed kilns and made charcoal. A purchase of seven empty tar barrels registered in the 1832 Lessebo bruk account book shows Falk began making tar. Building a tar kiln is a demanding task, and it often needed several tenants working together. An inventory of Jonas Peter's belongings shows that he also worked as a carpenter. In addition to several big axes and a small hand ax, he owned different kinds of saws and a carpenter's chest containing hammers, hatchets, grains, chisels, planes, a pair of compasses, various kinds of knives including five jackknives, a stave knife, a keyhole saw, as well as drills, augers, pliers, hooks and some other tools.

The Falk family lived a humble, mostly self-sufficient life. Jonas Peter also manufactured their furniture and all the wooden tools used in farming and in the household, including the plates and the spoons. The bedding was homemade and included cushions, beds with feathers for the parents and straw for the children, sheets, quilts, warm sheep pelts and bedspreads woven of wool, linen and hair from cattle. These were very prickly but wore well. At an early age the daughters learned to spin both wool and flax. They owned three spinning wheels and could spin for others to make a little extra income. Mother Anna Maria also taught her daughters how to weave, sew and knit. It was the women's duty to help in the fields and care for the hens, pig and cows. After the slaughter in December the meat was preserved by smoking or salting in tubs. In summertime the milk was carried in covered wooden buckets and churned into butter or made into cheese. On special occasions when there were eggs, milk and barley to spare, Anna Maria used the wafer-irons to make a treat or to bake Swedish pancakes on the foot-wide iron pan. When she brewed beer it was stored in a barrel Jonas Peters made.

After three years at the soldier's cottage Anna Maria, now 41, gave birth to a son Johan who died 3 months later.

Soon after the oldest daughter Lisa Stina was confirmed in 1835, she moved permanently to Furuby parish and lived with her maternal aunt and uncle. Her younger brother Anders and two sisters also were confirmed at age 15 but did not leave home to work as a farm hand and maids until they were 17. Their parents cared about and provided for their children until they were old and strong enough to cope with the hard working-life ahead of them.

The 19th and 20th century church books at times used comments like "old and infirm," "feeble," "disabled," and "incapable of working" to describe people over age 60. Jonas Peter and Anna Maria were now into their fifties and the day-work requirement for the soldier's croft started to wear them out. Soon all the children would leave home to make their own way. This meant less mouths to feed, but also a loss of teenage help. It was time to prepare for another way of life.

On a map from 1841 the rural country in Tollstorp along the road to Västorp looks like a quilt of irregularly shaped patches, consisting mainly of heather or bogs, but also of burn beaten land, pine groves and a few small enclosed fields. Here, Falk was able to rent four acres of land from Västregård. He built a cottage of hewn timber with bog moss as insulation to keep the cold and wind out. In 1843 Jonas Peter moved in together with his wife and their youngest daughter Lena Cajsa. Initially Falk's home was labeled as a backstuga which implies a dwelling without fields and meadows.

The family started clearing fields for rye and barley by removing stones and working the ground with grub hoes. A narrow strip of fertile soil produced root crops and flax. The rest of the meager land provided winter fodder for the cow. It was customary for sharecroppers who broke new land to get from one to six years free. Thereafter the rent was paid with day-work; but Falk preferred to pay in cash with money he earned as a carpenter. When the size of the cleared fields increased, Falk's place was named Västratorp (the Western croft) and he was referred to as torpare (*crofter, sharecropper*).

The cottage had curtains in both windows and was furnished with beds attached to the wall, a table, five simple chairs, a sofa and three cupboards. A clock, a mirror and one picture hung on the wall. For honored guests a linen tablecloth was placed on the table that could be set with three porcelain plates, six knives, four forks, three glasses, a candle holder and a glass bottle filled with liquor. The family owned 19 books, including one big Bible, two religious books of family sermons and 16 other books—more than most sharecroppers had.

Anna Maria cared for her family very deeply, was skillful and tidy and attended church regularly. As did other women of that era she used a spice box to keep awake during the ceremony. Her most important personal belongings reflect the circumstances in which she lived. Anna Maria owned several long shirts, six skirts, seven jackets and 16 headscarves.[4] She owned gloves and caps, but no shawl, no coat and no raincoat. She owned a pair of wooden shoes used for every-day-living at Västratorp, but also had leather shoes and a pair of boots.

Misfortune struck again and Anna Maria contracted a lung disease. By 1848 her condition deteriorated so badly that her youngest daughters returned home to nurse their mother and assist their father in running the croft. Sara Helena at age 23 was a sturdy and strong woman capable of doing a man's work in the fields. Her six-year-younger sister Lena Cajsa was also a hardy worker who previously had helped her father clear the land. She now took care of her mother and tended to the household.

The Falks had raised four children through good times and bad—for better and for worse. Now Jonas Peter did everything he could to cure his wife. He bought medicine and consulted a doctor, very uncommon for a sharecropper in those days. He intended to cover the cottage to make it warmer and healthier and started felling trees for that purpose. At the beginning of June 1848 he had 48 boards stored at the croft, ready to be installed.

But Anna Maria's condition deteriorated fast and on June the 18th Jonas Peter's beloved wife died at age 56. In the inventory after her death the largest debt recorded was 18 Rd. to Doctor Ekelund. As a monument to her diligence Anna Maria left five yards of linen cloth she created from seed to loom. [And48] Nearly two gallons of flax seeds remained—and was never sown.

The postmortem inventory showed a net debt. This meant Falk was not entitled to any widower's benefits and could only keep his bed and one set of bedding. The inventory value was underestimated by 30%-50%, (it always was, to help out the survivors) so at the auction it sold for more. There was a bit of money left over when everything was auctioned off. But with only these limited funds Falk had to buy back his chairs, tables, household utensils, carpentry tools, his cow and the boards he recently cut. He had to borrow money again to support everyday life and maintain his house.

According to the Swedish law, workers were contracted for a year and were only free to change employers during one single week in November. In the fall 1848 Jonas Peter's fortunes were still poor and Sara Helena and Lena Cajsa decided not to go back to work, but instead stay another year at Västratorp and care for their father.

At the nearby croft Gransholmen under Västragård lived farm maid Anna Helena Carlsdotter Streling with her family. Her health was poor and so were her parents. She was 35 years of age and had little chance to raise a family or have a home of her own. In some future scenario she could imagine herself as a pauper. On August 12th, 1849 Falk married Anna Helena. He was 19 years older than the bride and his children were not overjoyed. They had seen what happened when an old man without means married a much younger woman. Often when the husband died first, the widow and children were left needy and poor. At times the only way out was to be a beggar or a pauper. Around November 25th 1849 Falk's daughters Lena Cajsa and Sara Helena moved away from home; Lena to serve at an estate in Östra Thorsås and Sara to work on a farm in Furuby parish. Anna Helena Sterling was now in charge of the home.

Falk's life changed with a new wife of a fertile age. He felt rejuvenated and anticipated a second family. In 1850 Anna Helena gave birth to Hanna Mathilda and three years later another daughter Eva Charlotta was born. In the 1850s an individual over 60 often became worn out and unable to work. Falk no longer had the strength for daywork, but still had to pay the rent at Västratorp. He was surprisingly resilient and struggled on, working as a postman delivering mail to and from Tollstorp and tending beehives to sell the honey for extra money. He also used his carpentry tools and skills to take on sundry repair and construction tasks. But after five years of marriage time caught up with the debilitated couple. His strength and her health both deteriorated. He could not farm anymore and Västratorp reverted to a backstuga. The churchbook described him as "poor and indigent" and his wife as "sickly."

In May 1852 Falk's daughter Lisa Stina emigrated to Chisago Lake in North America, together with her husband Magnus Jonasson and their four children. Magnus also took his wife's sister Sara Helena and Carl Linn who was betrothed to Lena Cajsa Falk. That fall Magnus wrote a long letter home to Sweden, stating "if my father-in-law (Jonas Peter Falk) was not married, I would have brought him too." The following year Lena Cajsa also left Sweden to marry Carl at Chisago Lake. Of Falk's children by his first wife Anna Maria, only son Anders remained behind in Sweden.

At home at Västratorp things went from bad to worse. On July 11th, 1860 Anna Helena died from inflammation of the abdomen, eleven years after their marriage. Jonas Peter became a widower for the second time. The inventory in late October revealed he was in debt to Hovmantorp parish, the soldier's fund, some craftsmen and a number of private individuals. And a month later the annual croft assessment was due to Västragård. When Falk failed to pay the tax in November

1860 he lost the right to be a sharecropper and the land was incorporated with the farm.

According to family lore, Falk and his two daughters had to spend the winter of 1860/1861 in a root cellar previously used to store potatoes; but this seems unlikely. Falk was living under the jurisdiction of Juror Daniel Jonasson in Västragård, Magnus Jonasson's younger brother. It is inconceivable that Daniel would have let his brother's father-in-law and two small children to live in a cellar during the winter. That would have spoiled his good name. More likely Falk and the two girls were allowed to live in their little house for time being, but without land to farm or to keep a cow. Jonas Peter wrote about his miserable plight to his daughters Lisa Stina and Lena Cajsa and their husbands at Chisago Lake.

Falk greatest fear was to be a pauper. The 68-year-old man did everything he could to maintain his independence and pride. If he was given aid, the family would only get enough food to survive, but all his assets were to be confiscated and entrusted to the pauper fund. And in addition, being a pauper was stigmatizing. Jonas Peter's girls would end up at the bottom of the social ladder and could not expect to marry their way out of poverty. At the parish meeting on May 22th, 1861 "10 Rd. was donated from the emergency fund for Falk's children to attend

11.1: *The entrance to the potato cellar at "Falkalyckan" resembles a Munch scream. Photo: Ingvar Malmberg.*

school at Västratorp." This is the only record of Falk receiving any support. [Pro55]

Magnus Jonasson, along with Carl and John Linn at Chisago Lake, were sympathetic to the pitiful destitute and raised money to buy three tickets. June 1861, Jonas Peter Falk and daughters Hanna Mathilda, 11 and Eva Charlotta, 8 left for America.

At Västratorp the farmer cleared four acres into two fields separated by a broad stone fence. He also built a buried potato cellar with an arched roof. The 5½ feet thick walls of big stones left an inner dimension of 8×8 feet with 6 feet of headroom. This was the work of a man with strong farm hands and in need for a safe place to store potatoes near his new fields. Today the former clearing is wooded and named "Falkalyckan" (*Falk's enclosed clearing*). No evidence of a cottage remains, but the old impressive potato cellar still stands.

Falk spent the next 20 years with Carl Linn's family in Chisago County. This was the happiest time of his life. In appreciation Jonas Peter helped out wherever he could. He saw to it that the family firewood was split. When he was not working at the woodpile, he sat in the kitchen and knitted socks for all his children and grandchildren.

Falk enjoyed smoking a pipe and was very pleased when an Indian gave him some tobacco plants. Soon the old man had ample snuff and smoking tobacco. The finest leaves were carefully picked, well dried and then milled in a coffee grinder to a fine snuff. When he received compliments for its good taste he said smiling: "Ja, ja, I added a couple of drops of alcohol."

Falk did everything very quickly and he proclaimed pipe smoking did not have to be "the work of a lazy dog." He stuffed the pipe full of tobacco, lit it, and then smoked with a frenzy, disappearing behind a cloud of smoke. When the tobacco was finished, Falk knocked out the ashes on the stove, put down the pipe and declared: "Oh ja! Now I will knit stockings until bedtime!" Jonas Peter worked fast and he thought everyone else should be equally as energetic. One day as he stood by the woodpile chopping wood, Samuel Agrell,[5] an acquaintance from when he was in the old country, was driving by with a carriage drawn by two small mules. Such animals move very slowly when they are allowed to go as they please—and these mules moved at their own pace. Jonas Peter thought that if Samuel did not coerce the lazy beasts to go faster, he would not be home before dark. When the mules were near enough, Falk hurried down to meet Agrell: "Good day, Sammel—are

11.2: *Jonas Peter Falk 1793–1881.*
Photo: John Linn collection.

you coming—or going?" Jonas Peter asked and got a belly laugh in
reply. Quickly, he raised his birch-bark box, offered some snuff and
then hurried back to his woodpile. [Ten69]

In 1881 Jonas Peter Falk died in his daughter Lena Cajsa's home
at the age of 88. The old immigrant was buried in Glader's cemetery,
where he rests among relatives and friends. Half a century later, Vilhelm Moberg stood in front of his gravestone for a long time pondering
what had brought such an old man to leave his native land.

12

How an early emigrant returned home with nothing but sand

Swedish emigrants like Jonas Falk, Anders Peter Glader and Magnus Jonasson left their home in Småland for a new and better one in America. Home, surrounded by friends, relatives and like-minded individuals was very important to them. A significant number of the early settlers at Chisago Lake had known each other in Sweden. In America they tried to duplicate their former environment, but with more freedoms, opportunities and economic success than if they had remained in the old country. Despite all their struggles, they eventually became comfortable and happy with their new lives as Americans.

For some it didn't work out. If disillusionment, lack of prospects, separation from friends and loved ones or cultural difference became too much, they had to move again, often with the same apprehensions and struggles as before. Some moved west and some to Canada—and some even returned back to Småland. One Swedish-American who returned was Johan Linnell. He was clearly different from most, though the particulars and motives of his travels remain enigmatic.

Johan, Magnus Jonasson's older brother, was born Johan Jonasson in 1811 in Lambritsgård in Västorp. Maria Petersdoter, mother of Carl and John Linn was then a young girl living at the farm Amunsgård next door and Maria's parents Peter Månsson and Cathrina Johansdotter were witnesses at Johan's Christening.

In 1830 Johan moved to Växjö and became an apprentice to the cabinetmaker Schander. While still an apprentice, he started using "Linnell" as his surname. After four years of apprenticeship he traveled around as a journeyman carpenter. He became literally a "man on a journey," in keeping with his job description.[1] What he did and where he went in the 12 years between 1834 and 1846 is still a mystery and provides no clues to his motivation or character. He is not found in the Swedish records again until 1846 when Johan set sail for America.

For Smålanders, America and the promise of religious and economic freedom, equal opportunity and cheap fertile land were hard to ignore, though the travel to get there was long and dangerous and the cultural mores they would encounter were unpredictable. It took great courage to choose to emigrate into the unknown. It often required a strong sense of adventure, willingness to travel and motivation to improve ones life. Magnus Jonasson's older brother Johan Linnell surely had all these characteristics—and yet he was quite different too.

In Stockholm in July of 1846 Linnell boarded the ship Caroline headed for New York. He befriended a bunch of Janssonites following Erik Jansson to Illinois to help found Bishop Hill. But Johan himself never went there. After landing in New York, Johan's letters home surely influenced Magnus Jonasson to record Illinois as his destination on the passenger list when he immigrated in 1852. [Ado78]

When Johan arrived in New York, less than 2000 people living in the United States had been born in Sweden. Johan was in the vanguard of immigrants from Kronoberg county. His encouraging letters from New York to Magnus in Linneryd poked a hole in the dike that kept the disenchanted Smålanders in Sweden. The statement in the 1852 *Växjö Bladet*[2] "It is reported that some in the company have relatives in the Promised Land" surely points to Johan Linnell.

When Johan learned of Magnus' plan to immigrate he agreed to meet his brother in New York. Sadly Johan never showed—much to the concern of the party of new immigrants. What happened? Where was the American wife Johan said would be with him? [Tud11]

Johan's journey was far from over. Shortly after arranging via letter to meet Magnus, "gold fever" struck hard. Perhaps his next letter that changed the plans had arrived in Sweden too late and Magnus had already left for America; or perhaps the letter was lost; or never sent at all. Magnus was surprised and disappointed his brother was not there to greet him. He never saw his brother again. Johan set out for the new state of California before Magnus arrived.

Gold seekers from New York often went by ship to the gold fields, either around the tip of Cape Horn at the southern tip of South America—"around the Horn" as they called it—or by land across the Isthmus of Panama to the Pacific and then on to California by ship again. At its best, the Horn route took about 45 days and you could bring along a lot of supplies. The Panama route could be done in 30 days, but you had to travel light across the Isthmus. Travel directly across the entire US was very dangerous and could take 6 months or more. All routes were subject to many delays.

Johan arrived in over-crowded San Francisco in winter 1852–3, along with many other likeminded prospectors. One hundred thousand gold seekers from all over the world converged on the northern Sierra Nevada range. For most, their dreams never came true and desperation forced them to find other opportunities to get rich. Fortunately Johan's itching gold fever paid off. He reportedly made some money in the California goldfields—better than most. With gold in his pocket, he began to itch again.

In February 1851 gold was discovered in New South Wales in East Australia. Some of the men who went bust in California moved on to Australia in hopes of discovering the "mother load." Many of them rushed ashore in Melbourne. Like pack mules loaded with equipment, they trudged on foot to the gold fields carrying their tents, tools, pots, blankets and food on their backs. The prospectors suffered in the hot, dry Australian goldfields, sheltered only by tents or makeshift huts. During the day they worked under the merciless searing sun. Prices of food and other necessities rose to unimaginable levels. In the early years it was a lawless country where gangs of criminals constantly harried their victims. Later the poorest gold diggers could not afford to buy excavation permits, so the local sheriff fined them and threw them in jail. During the ten-year gold rush, the population of Australia tripled. In just three years Melbourne grew from 29,000 to 123,000 residents and tent cities popped up on the edge of town. The territory expanded quickly—and spread misery as it did. Replace the names Australia with United States and Melbourne with San Francisco, and it was the California Gold Rush all over again.

Johan, now on the Pacific coast, headed for Australia. Was it still gold fever, or just the most interesting way back to Sweden with his newfound wealth? The family story doesn't say. He did not return home for several more years, but he eventually made his way back to Sweden. Carl Vernon Swensson, Olof Linnell's grandson stated: "He spent years in Australia and later in Russia. His niece (Carolina Johanson[3]) told me that it was not true as reported by someone in America that he disappeared in Russia for he came back to Sweden and she knew where he was buried. He died in her father's home." [Lin05]

> The largest gold rush ever was in Russian Siberia. It started a couple of decades earlier, and continued at full strength for a few decades more. At that time in the late 1850s much of the gold came from mines along the Lena River in eastern Siberia, reachable via a trek of a few hundred miles from the Sea of Okhotsk on the Pacific coast. Like the other gold rushes of the period, many foreigners were attracted to the riches found in this inhospitable land. During its peak, Russia mined and smelted 40% of the world's gold.

Maybe Johan's wanderlust took him to Siberia in search of more gold. Itching again? After his Siberian experience, Johan probably would not have crossed Siberia-Russia to St. Petersburg, choosing instead to return to Sweden via the Indian Ocean and across the Isthmus of Suez—the easiest and safest route. A journey across Siberia at that time seems implausible, even for an experienced wanderer. The story of Johan Linnell still retains many mysteries.

He planned to return to his family in Sweden as a rich American, but after the arduous journey he was nearly penniless and terminally ill with consumption when he returned alone in 1862. He learned both his parents died while he had been wandering. Five months later at age 51 his itch finally stopped for good. The wandering enigma who was Johan Linnell died in Tollstorp Westregård, not far from where he was originally born.

Was Linnell like Karl Oskar's brother Robert in Moberg's *Emigrants* novels, a reticent dreamer accused of making up stories to hide his failures? Or was he the bold adventurer Robert who got everything he ever wanted—only to lose it all and become a disappointed and disillusioned traveler returning home to a brother skeptical of his success. His gold had turned to sand!

Magnus and Johan's brother Daniel did not emigrate. He made a permanent home in Sweden. However two of his children were adventurous and went to America. One returned to Sweden, while the other married and moved about a lot in America. Johan and Daniel were polarized cases, but other stories told by descendants of immigrant Smålanders describes picking up stakes and moving to gain a better life—occasionally every few months. How do we compare these other roaming Swedes with the eccentric and wandering first-born Johan and the stable and home-loving last-born Daniel?

13

About Glader's life after Elin's death, how he ended up out in the cold and his son's visits to the Great Lakes and down south

By late autumn in 1855 it had been two years since Anders Peter Glader arrived at Chisago Lake. He paid the highest of prices to reach his American dream. His two youngest daughters Fredrika and Petronella died along the way. His wife Elin could not cope with the trauma and tragedy of the journey and the extreme challenges of life in Minnesota Territory. After twenty years of marriage, Anders Peter was now a widower. While his sister Christina and her family were living with him the first winter, his brother-in-law Johan Håkansson was killed while cutting down trees. Johan had been one of his very best friends for over 20 years.

Glader's family produced little on the homestead that could be sold for cash. They lived on what they could make or grow. The farm could not supply them all and the families split.

Carl was 20 years old and Gustav 16 when their mother died and they had to provide for themselves. Anna Maria at age 15 had just been confirmed and was considered old enough to start serving as a maid. Christina stayed home and took care of the Glader household while her sons worked up north as lumberjacks in the big pine forests. When Anders Peter compared what he left in Sweden to what he gained in America, there wasn't much to celebrate. Their emigration felt like a catastrophe. Many others in the same situation would have been desperate or consumed with self-loathing. But Anders Peter knew there was only a way to go—and it was forward.

Gustav inherited his father's gumption and positive attitude. Right after the 13-year-old boy arrived at Chisago Lake he took a job on the Steamship "Old Enterprise" plying the Croix River to Taylors Falls. He became a cook's assistant and in the process was the first in the family to learn English, the language of his new country. In winter his older brother Carl worked as a lumberjack in the pineries up north and in the spring he drove the logs floating downriver to the mills. He worked outside in all weather disregarding the cold and the snow or the rain and the wind. He had to drag the heavy logs off the river bank into the water. If the timber jammed together on the river, the logs had to be separated before the logjam became too big. His clothes got wet from the rain and the snow and from falling into the river, but he could only let them dry while he still wore them. He was paid well for this backbreaking and dangerous work and in the spring of 1856, now 21, Carl bought 100 acres of his own land south of his father's homestead.

The two Glader brothers were aware of the new road under construction to connect St. Paul to the Great Lakes in the north and they learned that a wealthy businessman was investing a lot of money at the other end of that road at Lake Superior. A large city was to be established at one of America's best natural ports. The construction boom meant a hardworking man could earn a lot of money. Carl and Gustav followed the road to the Lakes in 1856. But the year after they arrived, the financial sector crashed in the northern states. Banks closed, money became worthless and personal finances were ruined. The population of 1200 soon diminished to only a few hundred people. Some of Carl and Gustaf's wages were seized in the resulting bankruptcies and never paid, so the brothers returned home.

There was always something going on back home at South Center Lake. Some young men not currently working used to hang out at Magnus Jonasson's farm just north of Glader's. This gang of boys-becoming-men had time to spare and would spin yarns, play cards, sing and otherwise entertain themselves just as they would in Småland. Gustav Glader, now age 19, was back home and unemployed with time on his hands so he decided to learn American English. At age nineteen he became a student in School District 10 in Chisago County. Here 38 students between the ages of four and twenty learned English.

After the disastrous year of 1854 when so many immigrants died of cholera, the flow of emigrants from Sweden to North America almost totally stopped. There were few single women in Chisago and many Swedish bachelors and widowers wanted a wife from the old country. In 1857 Gustaf Wiberg, living next door to the Lindahl family, traveled back to Sweden. Four years earlier, he had emigrated from Östra Thorsås. Now he returned home to escort his fiancé Maria Magnusdotter[1] from Hörda back to America. Her sister-in-law and nephew died of cholera after the 1854 Atlantic crossing on the bark Laurvig so Maria was understandably reluctant to make the long dangerous journey alone. When Gustav came to accompany her she screwed up her courage and emigrated in 1858, together with several others from the district.

By the fall of 1857 two years had passed since Elin's death. Glader wanted to remarry, but a poor fifty-year-old settler with a couple of half-grown children, was not high on the list of eligible bachelors. Anders Peter had always been fond of women and still felt full of life. Rather than marry a widow, he decided on marrying a strong, younger woman of childbearing age.

Anna Nord was born in Herråkra parish in 1831. She was the daughter of the soldier Anders Nord from soldier cottage 95 in Lilla Ryd. In the fall of 1850 she started working as a maid at Getingagården, very close to Furuby church. Many girls and boys changed employers every fall, but Anna quite enjoyed where she worked. After three years she was "with child" and in the summer of 1854 Johan August was born. He died suddenly two days after baptism. Most of the girls like this had to return home, but Anna was allowed to remain on the farm. In the fall of 1857, she became a maid for Erika Christina Holm, the widow of a priest in her home church in Furuby. Anders Ståhl was married to Glader's sister Lisa and they lived just across the road in soldier cottage 36. In March 1858, the young Anna Nord realized that she was "with child" again and on April 8 she received an exit permit to North America. There are more questions than answers; did the maid leave because she was pregnant, or had she planned the trip all along and her pregnancy was just the final farewell? The fact that Anna did not sign another one-year contract to be a maid on a farm in the fall of 1857 suggests that she planned to leave the following year. How could she afford to pay for the trip? Had Anna been saving for years to buy a ticket to America, or did the father of her expected child pay for the trip to avoid a scandal? Was it the same man as last time? When Anna arrived at Chisago, everyone could see that she would soon give birth. Again, many questions, few answers. How did she know where to go? Did the soldiers wife Lisa put in a good word with her brother Anders Peter, and did Anna agree to marry him? How did Glader respond to her pregnant condition?

On November 10, 1858, Anders Peter married the 25-year-younger Anna Nordström as she called herself in America. Three days after the wedding, Frans Emil was born and Glader accepted the baby boy as his foster son. Glader's fifteen-year-old daughter Lena Stina, proving to be as strong willed and energetic as her father, refused to accept the very pregnant Anna as her foster mother. Eight days before Glader's marriage, Lena Stina was married in the town of Vasa to Harrison Church, a middle-class American with British roots. She also Americanized her name to Helena Christine. The groom's father came from England where he was said to have been a circus performer. One year after her wedding a daughter named Wealthy Church was born in Marine Mills, 15 miles south of Glader's homestead.

The Swedes in Chisago strived to maintain their old country culture and now they sought a permanent teacher for their Swedish school. They created a committee to draw up plans for a teacher's residence and to estimate the work to build it. Three years earlier when the church selected the construction committee, Anders Peter's name was at the top of the list. But now in October 1858, his name was at the bottom below eight other men. What happened?

In the summer of 1858, the first Swedish Methodist revival meeting in Minnesota was convened in a beautiful grove of trees next to Glader Cemetery on the shore of South Center Lake. Four Methodist ministers led worship services over several days. The attentive crowd sat on simple plank benches in front of an outdoor pulpit, listening for many hours to prolonged sermons. During this revival, 21 people formed the Methodist Assembly of Chisago. Östgötlander Anders Svensson was one of the founders. He previously had been treasurer of the Church, but by 1856 had been ostracized from the congregation. Four immigrants from Älmeboda also participated in the meeting: John Elmqvist, his brother Nikolaus, their sister Maja Lena and her husband John Smith. In his book[2] Algot E. Strand mentioned his parents were also there and claimed more Methodist meetings were held on the shore of South Center Lake on Glader's property. Several Methodists were buried in Glader Cemetery before they had their own churchyard.

Many members of the Lutheran congregation of Center City were hostile toward other congregations. Sometimes as the Methodists came together to worship in their small church in Center City they were confronted by stone-throwing boys. One anecdote claimed the Lutheran priest in the pulpit cautioned against selling land to Methodists. Anders Peter Glader was a strong-willed and stubborn person who spoke his mind. No one would decide for him. By allowing Methodists to bury their dead in his cemetery, by providing a place for their revival meetings and by marrying a 25-year-old pregnant woman carrying another man's child, he challenged the mores of the Lutheran congregation.

In early 1857 America had an economic boom and in Sweden new emigrants were enticed by the bright prospects in Minnesota territory. The following summer, a group of 100 single young Smålanders arrived in Stillwater—only to learn an economic crisis had struck Minnesota. It was very difficult to get work. Many immigrants went south where the jobs were. In 1858 the only wages the Swedes in Chisago could get was a dollar a bushel for picking 150 bushels of cranberries.

Pastor Cederstam had not been paid his salary for three years and he resigned. The position remained vacant. In the absence of a priest, a church member read the sermons. The young people no longer met in the church but in the woods close by to enjoy freedom. In Sweden, most had been believers by tradition, without much reflection. Few had very strong convictions.

Sometimes pastor Peter Carlsson from Carver County or one of his colleague would visit and hold church services in Center City. They often stayed with Magnus Jonasson at Lönnö, only a little over a mile from the church by rowboat. Usually Magnus' son Olof rowed the priest back and forth.

> Peter Carlsson was born in Hjortsberga in Kronoberg county in 1822. During his teenage years he lost his faith in God and lived a wanton life, but his sole was saved a year after his wedding and then he became determined to convert others into believers too. With God's will, Peter and his wife Anna Stina emigrated to North America in 1854. They joined a group of 30 people, sailing from Gothenburg to Boston. In Chicago, half of them died from cholera. Peter helped to take care of the sick and to bury the dead. He and his wife fell ill, too. They had already loaned all their money to fellow travelers and now suffered dreadfully with no food or shelter. Pastor Erland Carlsson befriended this warm believer and encouraged him to spread God's word in his new homeland.

In 1857 Peter Carlsson and his wife moved to Carver County, Minnesota where he held evangelistic revival services for almost two years. After the economic crash, people were willing to listen to sermons about sin, revival and repentance.

Pastor Carlsson was a skilled revivalist and more and more of the young people in Chisago County were saved. At the beginning of August 1859, Magnus Jonasson's son Olof Linnell had a life-changing experience. He saw a girl who had often missed the church service in favor of dancing with other young folk, but now she was kneeling in the pew with her hands together while reading the Lord's prayer. During the service, pastor Carlsson challenged the congregation "How long can you remain in the company of the godless and ignore the grace God revealed through Christ?" Olof felt this was addressed directly at him and from that moment forward, he would become saved.

In the summer of 1859, Carl and Gustav Glader together with Olof Linnell decided how they might earn a living. The financial crisis was less severe in the southern states. The plantation owners sold cotton to England with payment in gold. The young men decided to go south. Six young Kronobergers seeking work departed from Chisago to St. Paul to travel by steamboat down the main artery of America, the Mississippi River. They went to St. Louis in Missouri and continued further south.

The wealthy southerners in their elegant colorful clothes and lace and ruffled adornments were a striking contrast to the immigrants in their old and dreary travel clothes. The unemployed men could only afford steerage class on the lower deck among the beggars, pigs and cargo. After a total of twenty days and 1700 miles, the immigrant Swedes arrived at Grand Gulf, a bustling port on the river in the state of Mississippi. From here in the south, cotton from the plantations was shipped north in a busy exchange of goods with the northern states. The day after the Smålanders arrived they witnessed a slave auction— an experience none of them would ever forget. Olof Linnell described what they saw:

> Among those sold was a distraught slave woman with two children. When she was sold she pleaded for the man who bought her to buy her children as well. But, no consideration was given to her prayer and the oldest child was sold to another. When the second child was offered for sale, the poor woman fell down on her knees in front of the man who owned her, crying with tears she prayed as hard as a heartbroken mother could pray for him to buy her child too. But the man displayed no sympathy and his answer was: "Shut up you black ... "

This image will never leave my memory as long as I live. [Lin05]

The Smålanders ended up in St. Joseph, Louisiana. The city is located on the banks of the wide and muddy Mississippi River. From there it flows slowly past New Orleans on to the Gulf of Mexico. The surrounding land is barely above the river and contains many ponds and larger sausage-shaped lakes that have been formed over thousands of years as the river changed course. Mosquitoes were a constant irritant and malaria a common disease. The summers were oppressive from heat and high humidity, while the winters were mild and rainy. The Swedes were skilled lumberjacks and just outside St. Joseph the young men found work. Carl Glader and his comrades earned a dollar for every cord of firewood harvested. The logs were cut 1-1½ feet long to fit kitchen stoves and riverboat boilers. After seven months of hard work, the Småladers earned 200 dollars each. And while staying here they had a new revelation. The journey south taught them what slavery meant. They realized America was a country with extreme class differences. As poor menial workers from the North, they were often insulted and despised by the rich aristocratic southerners with their refined manners.

The young men did not go to church because there was no Swedish-speaking Lutheran church in St. Joseph. Olof had packed his book of Psalms, a Bible and a big book of sermons in his travel bag. He read them at every opportunity to better understand the words of the Bible. He also yearned for more education. In the old country he learned to read and write Swedish. In America he could speak English, but not write it.

When the six young men returned to Chisago Lake, Carl Glader bought more land. He now owned over 140 acres, more land than his father. In order to earn cash necessary to develop the land, Carl and Gustav had to drive logs on the river and work in the mills. In the winter they logged the big pine forests up north. Times were still tough.

14

About the rise and fall of a member of the parliament and two sisters buried at Glader's cemetery

In 1962 linguist Folke Hedblom visited many Swedish settlements in North American searching for old Swedish dialects. He was drawn to the Swedish-American community surrounding the old Indian lake Ki Chi Saga in Minnesota. Hedblom interviewed many descendants of immigrant Swedes, capturing their stories and speech patterns with his tape recorder. Some spoke in the same Småland dialect their immigrant ancestors spoke more than a century earlier. Others used a mixture of Swedish and American English (Swinglish) to tell their story.

"I was born here on the southern shore of Center Lake. One of my neighbors was named Carl Linn and another was named Glader" said 78-year-old Arvid Carlsson into Folke Hedblom's recorder. Arvid's great-grandfather, Magnus Jonsson lived in Ormeshagahult in Hovmantorp parish in Småland and had been a member of the Swedish Parliament under King Karl XIV Johan. Since his family was considered quite wealthy Arvid always wondered why his grandfather and grandma emigrated. [Car62] But Arvid didn't know. He heard many stories from the old country, but none about the family's rise and fall that brought his forefathers to America.

In 1810 Magnus Jonsson and his wife bought her parent's farm in Ormeshagahult village in Hovmantorp. He served as a juror at the King's District Court for many years and in the parliament in Stockholm for a short time. Because Magnus had a very good reputation, he was appointed manager of the parish granary after a previous discrepancy in the accounts had been discovered. Several years later, the inspector from Lessebo launched a second audit—commissioned by none other than Bergsrådet Aschan. The investigation showed 600 Rd. missing and Magnus Jonsson was sued and summoned before the court. His reputation and honor and hence the family's future was at stake.

For many hundreds of years "hedern och äran" was one of the most important values of Swedish society. Both "heder" and "āra" can be translated as "honor" in English. Heder is something intrinsic within an individual. An honorable person has his own code of honor. This honesty then grants him/her trust and appreciation. This person is honored (ärad) by others. Hedern och äran had to be cultivated and defended. Honorable actions increased a man's honor, while dishonesty decreased it. A person with a good reputation could become a member of a clique that could improve one's social position. He who behaved dishonorably risked being ostracized. In the middle of the 19th century hedern och äran still was a guiding principle for individuals, when judging their own and others actions. An honorable person was also honest and never lied or stole. When honorable men or women testified under oath, they told the whole truth and nothing but the truth.

For the government, reputation and honor were aspects of law. A person convicted of a dishonorable crime would lose both his honor and his civil rights. He was shunned by society and often lost his job. It was essential for a man to keep his honor and protect his family; but if he wasn't respected he could not protect and defend his name and family.   [Lin08]

As a former parliamentarian, Magnus ranked high on the social ladder. If he lost the case it would be devastating.

Magnus Jonsson testified under oath in the King's District Court that nothing improper had occurred. He said many of the identified discrepancies included accounting errors made before his appointment and the accrued interest on the resulting fictitious losses exacerbated the problem—interest on losses for transactions that never happened. He did agree that the procedures at the granary were less than adequate. He admitted that in situations when too many people simultaneously returned borrowed corn to the granary, he forgot to record some transactions due to the confusion. The money had been duly dispersed and was not "missing." He also argued that the Parish Assembly never required any receipts or credit records; the words of an honest man were sufficient. If receipts had been mandated for all transactions, this situation never would have occurred.

Magnus Jonsson felt wrongly accused but wanted to defend his "heder och āra" and do the right thing. To reach an honorable deal, he borrowed 666 Rd. to repay the claimed losses, using the farm in Ormeshagahult as collateral. [Maga37] In those days it was common to use promissory notes as if they were money. Often these credit declarations were exchanged as payment from one person to another. Only three weeks after the loan was initiated Magnus' debt agreement changed hands and now was held by someone else. You never knew who your loans would end up with ...

In 1833 Magnus Jonasson's elder son Johan married Lena Jonasdotter and took ownership of a small farm in Öljesholm in Linneryd. She was nine years his senior and had three children. In 1839 Johan and Lena sold their property and bought his father's farm in Ormeshagahult, because Magnus was delinquent on his 666 Rd. loan. Johan assumed his father's note, paid him some additional money and agreed to support Magnus and his wife for the rest of their lives. For the next three years Johan and Lena managed to run the farm with the help of Johan's siblings and several maids and farmhands. They were able to pay both the interest and the amortized principal on the loan. But in February 1842, the family was dealt a fatal blow—Lena contracted "a severe cold.[1]" and died from a high fever. Johan had to take out additional loans to provide the children with their inheritance. Soon the economic situation became untenable and he had to liquidate.

Bergsrådet Aschan had long coveted forested land near Lessebo forge and aggressively tried to buy Omeshagahult; but Johan Magnusson refused to sell to the man who had ruined his family. Instead on January 4, 1844 he sold the farm to David from Ekeberga for 2333 Rd. However, the owner of record ironically turned out to be one Johan Lorentz. David Johansson had merely been a "front man" selling the farm to Bergsrådet just two weeks after he bought it. Through this deception J. L. Aschan came in possession of the first of Ormeshagahult's four farms. [Magb36] Johan Magnusson had children, siblings and elderly parents to support so he swallowed the injustice, bowed his back and agreed to be yet another of Aschan's tenant farmers. On March 25, 1844 he became the tenant administrator on his father's old estate. Johan paid rent to Aschan in part through day work normally performed by a farmhand and the rest by hauling goods and equipment to and from the seaports. Johan also had to maintain the buildings and fences as well as tend to the forests and fields. In addition to his obligation to Aschan he continued to support and feed his parents. [Magc36]

Carl Zackrisson and his wife owned a fine farm in Ormeshaga with good forest and 5½ acres of rich and fertile fields with black soil. The lakes and wetlands provided winter fodder for nine head of cattle, equal number of sheep and a horse. But Mr. and Mrs. Zackrisson were in debt to Bergsrådet who forced them to sell out. Their old residence was demolished and the destitute family, including 12 children, were forced to live in a backstuga. They became beggars. In addition to being a tenant on his former farm, Johan Magnusson now became the tenant farmer on the former Zackrisson land as well. This additional lease increased the amount of freight he hauled to the seaports and significantly increased the number of days his farmhands and maids worked at Aschan's farm. Charcoal production for Lessebo forage became Magnusson's primary source of income. Days missed and freight not delivered further increased the debt owed to the Lessebo corporation. For Johan—as for many others—"They owed their soles to the company store." [Tra46]

In 1847 Bergsrådet bought the two remaining farms in Ormeshagahult and thus acquired an additional 1500 acres of forest. During the first half of the 1800s, the iron mills in Kronoberg county bought many farms to insure a supply of wood and charcoal. When Aschan took over the Lessebo forge in 1802 he owned six mantal of forested farms in Hovmantorp parish. Now 50 years later, he owned six times as much land in that parish alone, as well as farms, mines, ironworks, glassworks and paper mills all over Kronoberg, creating the mightiest industrial corporation in Småland at the time.

Also Samuel Agrell at Öljeslycke in Ormeshagahult was in debt and had to sell his farm to Bergsrådet. With the proceeds Agrell paid his debt to Johan Magnusson. Johan now saw a chance to escape. In 1851 he produced enough charcoal to earn 107 Rd., which enabled him to repay the entire debt to Aschan. [Afr17] The tenant farmers Samuel and Johan longed for a life with a better future and decided to leave for North America. In 1852 Magnusson repaired the buildings and the fences, cleared weeds and brush, fertilized, sowed and replanted everything to avoid any liability for improper maintenance.

Four years after his first wife's death, Johan married Lisa Mathisdotter from Wida Norregård in Ljuder. In 1853 his family consisted of the 19-year-old twins from the first marriage plus two daughters ages 6 and 3 and Carl Magnus, an infant son born in mid April. On May 25, 1853 Johan terminated his contract at Ormeshagahult and departed

Hovmantorp, never to return. On the voyage to America the family was joined by Lisa's sister Anna Stina Mathisdotter from Ljuder. She was 25, honest, had a good reputation and certified free to marry by the parish council. Anna Stina received a travel certificate from the priest after presenting authorization from her mother and brother agreeing to let her travel abroad.

His contemporaries described Aschan as everything between God our Father and His evil twin, the Devil. The *Swedish Biographical Dictionary* chronicles how Johan Lorentz Aschan established schools and hospitals and how in every way he worked to better the lives of his subordinates and improve public institutions. Bergsrådet also was a prohibitionist and a patron of higher learning. However the opinions of Aschan were divided and many of the common people considered him to be an evil and greedy man. Even today in Ormeshagahult the legend persists about how Aschan had sold his soul to the Devil and several 19th century tales describe how he was subjected to an exorcism. One goes like this:

> Since Bergsrådet Aschan was considered to be under the Devil's dominion, Reverend Peter Andersson from Hovmantorp was summoned. As he arrived and walked in to Bergsrådet's room, the dean saw not one but two people, both looking alike. He couldn't tell who was the Devil—and who was Aschan. So the priest drew a large circle on the floor and in it wrote "Our Father," urging both men to step into the ring. But the Devil couldn't do that. Instead the walls began to shake and crack and the Evil One fled ...   [And52].

In Hovmantorp and in Ljuder many who had read Magnus Jonasson's long letter from Ki Chi Saga decided to follow him. Eight families plus seven unmarried individuals emigrated from Hovmantorp in 1853. Many of them came from Ormeshaga and most went to Chisago Lake. Johan along with two other large families settled in Scandia in Washington County. There Johan Magnusson built a new cabin near Hay Lake. Sister-in-law Anna Stina Mathisdotter eventually married John

Lindgren, one of the passengers on the ill-fated bark Laurvig in 1854.
For many years, the families lived close together around Hay Lake.

Johan Magnusson's younger brother Carl was born in 1820 and by
1858 he was married to Glader's niece Anna Jonasdotter from Nyäng in
Västorp. The family lived modestly as tenants on a small farm named
Lundsdal under Ormeshaga.

Anna's mother Martha Andersdotter and her second husband Johannes also were tenants on the unassuming farm Nyäng in Västorp.

Martha's first husband was Jonas "Glader" Nilsson, older brother
of A, P. Glader. The two brothers had enjoyed life; a bright future was
palpable. Suddenly in 1826 Jonas was no more... But nineteen-year-
old Anders Peter rejected sorrow and continued living as before, full of
pranks and good stories, while maintaining the same joyous laughter.
Soon he too assumed the nickname "Glader." Jonas' daughters Maria
and Anna at Nyäng, now fatherless, had a close relationship with their
uncle Anders Peter living at the adjacent farm Berget. Thanks to him
their lives took turns that no one could have imagined.

After a year as a widow, Maria and Anna's mother Martha Andersdotter remarried. The new couple became successful tenants and had
some money to lend to others at the usual 5% interest. By the terms of
their contract the couple could remain securely in the same place for
their entire lives.

After having been confirmed Jonas and Martha's girls left home to
work as maids on farms in different parishes. Ten years later Maria
returned to help her mother and to take care of her aging grandfather
who had moved in with them. Anders Ståhl had been a cavalry soldier,
a tenant and a farm foreman—a man of good reputation. The family rejoiced when Maria in December 1850 married another cavalry soldier,
Carl Sandberg. When Carl was one year old his father, infantry soldier
Sven Storm in Ormeshagahult, drowned at the age of 22. The widow
was evicted and relegated to a remote cottage in the woods to make a
living in some way or other. Life had many setbacks.

In 1852, typhoid fever ran rampant and the family was hit hard.
At the end of November, their 18-year-old daughter succumbed. Two
weeks later on New Year's Eve their 24-year-old son died, followed by
their youngest daughter. Martha never recovered from this devastating
blow. She slowly deteriorated and finally died from tuberculosis at age

54, leaving only a husband and a daughter. In less than four years, this honest and hard-working family was nearly wiped out.

Anna Jonasdotter no longer wanted to remain in Sweden, a country with no prospects. As her discouragement reached bottom, she received a letter from her uncle Anders Peter Glader in Minnesota. He wrote "here you get land for free · · · you do not have to pay anything for the land." [Car62] Anna could not stop thinking about his claim and finally she convinced her husband to leave for Minnesota. In the spring of 1858, Carl and Anna sold everything they owned and set off with their three children; Johan 8, Helena 5 and Lovisa 3. They headed for Carl's older brother Johan Magnusson at Hay Lake.

About 100 years later Arvid Carlsson told Folke Hedblom about his grandmother Anna and grandfather Carl's long journey:

> A horrible storm struck them on the North Sea. The ship was close to sinking. Then my grandmother had no chance to turn around and go back... it was too late ...

> From England the family sailed across the Atlantic and arrived in New York after a little more than eleven weeks. They didn't arrive at Stillwater until September 20th and it was turning cold.

> First they stayed briefly with their grandfather's brother while they built a log shanty, or "stockhydda" as they call it in Swedish. The only tools available were an ax and a hammer. In those days they had no saw. Back then everything was done with an ax · · · In the spring of 1859, Carl would go out and hunt prairie hens. By then he acquired an old shotgun. It exploded when he first used it. He was clobbered on the side of his head and was unconscious for several days. Then he eventually regained conscience and recovered, but not completely and he died a year later. [Car62].

In the spring of 1860 Anna Jonasdotter gave birth to Elof and now was a widow raising four children in a foreign country. The only option she could think of was to go to Chisago Lake where her relatives lived. Anna moved in with Aunt Christina and her cousins Carl and Frans. The eldest son John (Johan) Carlsson was 10 and was to live with the

Anders Peter Glader family. At that time most neighbors owned two-to-four cows that grazed freely. Every evening eight to ten neighbors took turns rounding up the cattle and bringing them to their respective homes to be milked. When it was Glader's turn, he usually sent John to collect the cows. Sometimes the boy found them foraging nearby but at other times they ranged as much as four miles south. From the big herd of 300 cattle, he gathered the cows belonging to his neighbors and then drove them home. He started at four o'clock in the afternoon and some nights he was not home till nine. [Car62] John lived with the Gladers until he was confirmed at age 16 and considered an adult who could earn his own bread.

Anna Jonasdotter married Carl Lindahl. He was 31 years old and Anna was five years older. Together they had sons Frank and Solomon and a daughter Martha Christina. Carl Lindahl is to the left holding a cigarette in his right hand. Anna Jonasdotter Lindahl is standing in the back with her arm on Carl's shoulder. Frans Lindahl is on the right.

14.1: *The Lindahl family. Photo: Kathleen Pullen.*

Arvid Carlsson continues:

> Those who came here usually wrote back home saying you get land for free, but the actual price was really 1 dollar 25 cents an acre, still pretty cheap. They wanted to attract emigrants to live here. But after the newcomers arrived, they had a really hard time. Later, prices rose to as much as five dollars an acre. But that was next to the lake where everybody wanted to live and be able to fish and so on. In those early years they shot a lot of deer. This was a grand paradise for the deer. The whole forest

was practically full of them. One winter my grandpa
Carl Lindahl shot 35 deer and hung them up in a shed
outside. They froze solid. Then in the spring he would
skin them and tan the hides as well as he knew how.
They made sewn shirts and pants out of the hides, but
when it got wet, it scraped and shrieked when you
walked, because they could not tan them properly as
they do now. My dad said, "I got sick and tired of
wearing those deerskin pants because when they got wet
you could hear them a half-mile away."

Arvid also mentions that his grandmothers Maria and Anna were
sisters. Living in Sweden they had a close bond and Anna nourished
a dream that Maria and her family would settle at Chisago Lake. Then
"the great famine of Sweden" occurred in 1867 and 1868. The first year
crops failed due to cold weather and the next year failed again from
extremely hot and dry conditions. Though starvation was widespread,
the high and mighty authorities gave no aid and poor people died by
the thousands. Within three years 80,000 Swedes emigrated to North
America.

In 1869 Maria Strandberg and her family were ready to go too; Carl
had been allowed to resign from the Cavalry and Maria had no child
to nurse. According to the church records they were due to leave on
November the 11th, but the following year we find the family living as
tenants on the big farm Södregård in Hemmessjö parish. Probably this
was an offer they could not resist. The farm could feed as many as 12
heads of cattle through the winter, but Carl and Maria after some time
realized that they barely broke even due to the high tenant fee. After
six years the family moved to Växjö and continued to be tenants, but
now on smaller farms.

Anna and Maria never gave up the common dream of uniting their
families. In 1880 Maria's daughter Johanna Charlotta emigrated at the
age of 24 to Chisago Lake and moved in with the Lindahl family. Her
cousin John Carlsson had emigrated in 1859 and the two married in
1881 and had a son Arvid, our informant. In the following years Johanna's sister and a brother arrived and finally in 1888, Carl Sandberg
and his wife Maria emigrated with a daughter and a married son with
his family. They settled on a little farm in Chisago County.

At Glader Cemetery by the shore of Chisago Lake, Maria and Anna
were reunited for the last time. In January 1899 Maria Sandberg was

buried here, followed by her husband half a year later. So were Carl Lindahl and his wife Anna in 1911. Through the years thousands of tourists have been visiting this place of final rest for Maria and Anna from Nyäng. People from far off places have quietly read their names on the gravestones, without knowing what life had in mind for these two sisters from distant Småland.

15

About everyday life and Native American visits at Porter's Point

By 1855 Glader's sister Helena and her husband Anders Jaensson were looking forward to a prosperous life together. After purchasing more land in the Swedish settlement at Chisago Lake they now owned 189 acres.

Anders was first called "Anders at Porter's place" to distinguish him from all the other Jaensson, Johnsson, Jonasson, Johannesson and Johansson names of immigrants also living in the area. In the end the family simply adopted the surname Porter. As an old man Frank Porter, Anders and Helena's oldest surviving son, wrote down many of the stories he had been told about creating the early settlement and a great deal about his experiences during those times.

Helena and Anders Porter had seven children together. Their first-born were twins, a boy and a girl; but the girl was stillborn or died immediately after birth. The baby boy lived long enough to be named Carl Adolph and baptized before he also died. He was buried in Glader's Cemetery.

To grow crops the settlers had to clear hardwood forests and a dense undergrowth of brush, a hard and tiring job. After felling the trees it took them between five and ten years to dig up and dispose of the remaining stumps and roots. The earth was very fertile and the newly tilled fields produced fine harvests of corn, potatoes, rutabagas, beans, grain and kitchen vegetables. These together with bread, butter, cheese, milk and meat, were the staples of their larder.

To make coffee they roasted the beans at home; but instead of grinding them in a mill, they crushed them with a large round bottle. Then they mixed the crushed coffee with roasted rye. Maple syrup might be added to the brew if they wanted it sweetened. There were plenty of fish in the lake and children did most of the fishing. They twisted a homespun flax rope twice around the end of a rod and tied a hook made from an ordinary nail to the other end. Sometimes they fished using nets or by trolling.

As the family grew the log cabin became too small and Anders Porter then built a two-story house of hewn logs.[1] In the spring of

146

1860 after having lived there for only a single winter, the house burned down. Mother Helena carried 1½-year-old Frank out through a room full of fire and flames, laid him on the ground to be lifted up by his big sister Johanna who carried him away to safety. Helena returned to the rear of the house, knocked in a window and climbed in to rescue a couple of large Swedish chests containing bedding and other dry goods. Everything else in the house became prey to the flames. The family returned to the old cottage close to the stable where they continued to live until 1869 when Porter built a new more suitable house.

> Father sometimes did some carding evenings, otherwise this work usually devolved to my mother. The writer does well remember how she, after having tucked us little ones away for our night's sleep, often kept the spinning wheel humming until near midnight. For outside clothes white warp and black filling was ordinarily used, and for underwear white was used exclusively. When weaving was completed a tailor was hired to come to the house and make the men's suits and the underclothes were made by my mother. All sewing was made by hand. The weaving loom in which this cloth was made is now in the possession of the writer. [Por32]

There were no natural hayfields on Porter's property. Like many other farmers Frank's father harvested most of his hay on the banks of the Sunrise River nearly six miles away. In winter they dragged the hay home with a team of oxen. This was often difficult when driven snow formed large drifts, occasionally several feet high and they had to shovel to open the road. Frank sometimes accompanied his father on these trips. As his father pitched up the hay he would trample it down to compact it. They usually ate lunch of bread, homemade butter and cheese before starting back home. At times their food was frozen. It would have been nice to have had some hot coffee to dip it in and thaw it out a bit, but Frank had strong teeth and was hungry so he managed to eat it cold. His father soon tired of bringing in hay this way and reduced his herd of cows so the farm alone could feed them.

About the same time Anders Porter hired someone to cut the maple trees into cordwood as he cleared a new field. For this he paid one dollar per cord. The following winter the wood was taken by ox team to Taylors Falls and either sold for two dollars a cord, or traded for

15.1: *Anders Jaenson Porter*
Photo: Sven Adolfson.

15.2: *Helena Nilsdotter Porter*
Photo: Sven Adolfson.

goods worth two and a half dollars a cord. Around this time the family bought their first kerosene lamp. Kerosene cost a dollar per gallon but the quality was higher than we see today. It was a fire hazard and had to be handled carefully. As newly arrived immigrants, they dimly lit the living room with homemade tallow candles, and when they ran out they only had the glow from the open fireplace.

During the early years at Chisago Lake Chippewa Indians roamed the forests. In the early morning the settlers would hear rifle shots as the Indians hunted ducks by the lake. After mother Helena baked bread one day several Indians showed up at the house. They were carrying ducks and partridges to exchange for food. Using sign language they pointed to two loaves of bread as they placed the quail on the table. Mother Helena understood what was meant and handed them some bread. The Indians went on their way and were never seen again. "These Indians were very friendly and never did any harm to people or stock." Frank Porter remarked. The white settlers called them the "Chippewa," but the Indians referred to themselves as the "Ojibwe" or "Anishinaabe." Before the settlers arrived, the Ojibwe were free people who roamed their territory as they pleased. The forests were their

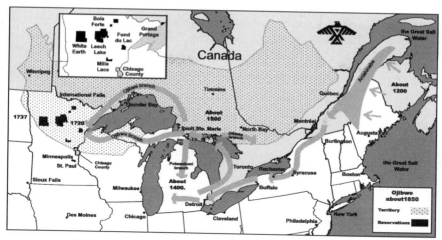

15.3: *Ojibwe Migrations from 1200 AD*   Map: *John Linn.*

home and the water provided both transportation and food. The pioneers arrival dramatically changed all that.

A thousand years ago, all the Anishinaabe lived on the shores of the "Great Salty Water" far to the east. For unknown reasons they broke up into smaller tribes that over time drifted southwest, first reaching the St. Lawrence river around 1400 BC. One of the tribes, now known as the Ojibwe first established a settlement at the rapids between Lake Superior and Lake Ontario. There they met French fur trappers and missionaries and traded fur for guns and gunpowder. With enhanced weaponry they spread their territory both south and west. Their expansion was finally abated in mid Minnesota by the Dakota tribes, their sworn enemies. During the 1850s the Government forced both the Ojibwe and the Dakotas off their traditional lands to live on reservations—with many broken promises that they could continue to hunt and fish on parts of their old hunting grounds. However, when many homesteaders arrived, wild game became scarce and the Ojibwe were forced to trade their lands for survival. Even so, the Swedish pioneers would occasionally meet and sometimes trade with Ojibwe visiting Chisago Lake.

At the end of the 1850s, things were changing; and not for the better. Although neither the Indians nor the Swedes realized it at the time, the Civil War was brewing—a war that would change all their lives forever. But that is another story for another day.

Endnotes

About a poor Östgötlander who came to be a settler · · ·

1. Micaela Leonarda Antonia de Almonester Rojas y de la Ronde, Baroness de Pontalba (b. 1795-d. 1874) was a Spanish aristocrat businesswoman and real-estate developer.
2. Fredrika Bremer (b. 1801 d. 1865) was a Swedish author and feminist.
3. Queen Margareta 1353-1412 reigned over Sweden including Finland, Norway, Denmark,Greenland, the Farrow Islands, the Shetland Islands and the Orkney Islands.
4. "King of the stumps" was a nickname his admirers gave him because of his strength and energy.

How Magnus Jonasson emigrated from Linneryd · · ·

1. Both the fictional Karl Oskar and the real Magnus Jonasson organized their respective parties of emigrants at Åkerby Junction.
2. Konga härad was a judicial district covering 15 parishes with the courthouse in Ingelstad.
3. An exit certificate is like a modern passport or visa. Unlike today's passports that allow the bearer to enter a foreign country, the exit visa was instigated primarily to insure that the citizens remained in or came back to Sweden. Also, before 1860, every citizen had to have another certificate to move to a different parish and register with the clergy there. This allowed the state to keep tabs on the movements within the country and discourage the increasing number of poor people from wandering around and begging. Beginning in 1860, both kinds of visas were no longer required until the 20th century.
4. Mantal is a measure of the wealth of a farm used for taxation purposes. It is not just a simple unit of area as it depends on the productivity of the land and other factors. In many ways the Swedish social and economic structures were quite different from those of America, as was the assignment of names to people and places. The volume *Swedish Roots* provides a more extensive vignette into life in Sweden prior to the mass emigration to America.

5. The Riksdaler Banko is similar to the German dollar of the time (Thaller); often abbreviated Rd. In those days the Rd. was roughly about the same as $5 in US currency at the time, but exchange rates varied widely depending on the relative financial situation in the US and Sweden.

6. Matts Hansson was the father of Hans Mattson (b. 1832, d. 1893), an early pioneer to Minnesota and later a famous Minnesota politician. Hans spent a year in Boston while corresponding with his family in Sweden. He convinced his father to join him in America the following year. Matts' voyage with Magnus Jonasson triggered a chain of events ultimately bringing many Swedes to Chisago County.

7. The sternwheeler was probably "The Queen of the Yellow Banks," which started regular service three days a week to Taylors Falls earlier that year. It was only 45 feet in length and had sufficiently shallow draft to avoid running aground on the treacherous passage from Stillwater.

8. Kyrktagning loosely translates to "a mother's absolution." It is an old church tradition in which God forgave the sins of the new mother and the priest accepted her back into the worship community.

9. Lönnö translates to "Maple Island." Lake levels are now lower and Lönnö has become the peninsula named Sunset Point.

10. "Big" probably referred to "long winded," not "prodigious." His grammar, syntax and spelling were poor, typical of the limited education commoners received in those days.

11. A crofter is a Swedish tenant farmer living and working on a farm owned by someone else. The crofter is responsible for managing and maintaining the farm, growing crops and providing a specified amount of day-work to the owner.

12. A backstuga (*hill cottage*) is a small, rural house with little or no land to farm and usually occupied by paupers, craftsmen or day-workers who do not own the property.

13. The crown tax was levied by the monarchy, not by the local government or the Church.

14. Magnus got his Indian names confused. He actually meant "the city of Oquawaka." Oquawaka is on the Illinois side of the Mississippi River, due west of Knoxville, The name Oquawaka was derived from the native peoples' word "Oquawkiek" meaning "Yellow Banks." Coincidentally, when Magnus first visited Taylors Falls he likely boarded the small sternwheeler "Queen of the Yellow Banks" that had

just started its Stillwater to Taylors Falls run about the time the Smålannders arrived from Oquawaka.

15. Basswood is related to the Linden tree, a favorite of the Swedes.
16. He had no cows that winter, but he is suggesting that if he did have two cows, he could have fed them. This is the salesman at his best.
17. A handbill is similar to a promissory note. The Swedes deposited cash with Liljeqwist for safekeeping and the handbill was the receipt. Then in New York the captain would exchange the handbill for the equivalent in American dollars and return it to the passengers.
18. His wife's foster parents had owned ⅜ of Kuppramåla in Linneryd parish. They sold it in part to raise money for Magnus and Lisa's emigration to America.
19. They had been eating poor and limited food for months and they were not used to the different microbes in the new country.
20. Jonas Peter Falk was the father of Magnus' wife Lisa.
21. The "Pineries" were along the St. Croix north of Taylors Falls.
22. Perhaps he was referring to "dark" Sweden where everything was repressed.
23. Having sold their farm, Johannes Andersson and Martha Bengtsdotter moved to Vide at the same time Magnus emigrated.
24. Anders Falk was Lisa's older brother. Anders later died from consumption in 1868. His wife Ingri and their five boys immigrated to Chisago Lake in 1869 in a desperate struggle for survival. They first lived with Carl Linn and then moved to their own place in Chisago Lake and called it Julatorpet after the farm they left in Hovmantorp. After a few years, they moved to a new homestead in Groton, South Dakota

How Carl from Linnehult took the name Linn · · ·

1. Carl probably met the Noreen family in Ormeshaga. The Noreens also emigrated to Chisago Lake and their descendants in America intermarried with the Linn family several times.
2. As a young girl, Carl's mother Maria Petersdotter lived next door to Magnus Jonasson. That connection eventually introduced Carl to Magnus and the Falks and Maria probably arranged for Carl to go to America with Magnus.

3. In some later years census takers who came from other parts of Sweden entered the name in the census as they heard it. They incorrectly spelled the name "Lind," the more common Swedish spelling.

4. The farm Amundsgård has a history back into the 16th century. The farm Lambritsgård where Magnus Jonasson was born is adjacent to Amundsgård and the two houses were only a couple hundred yards apart.

5. Jonas Svensson, Magnus Jonasson's father also came from Näsby. It is likely that Jonas Svensson knew Jonas Andersson's family and perhaps arranged the marriage to Maria Petersdotter.

How Glader emigrated with family and followers · · ·

1. Fardag (*day of coming and going*) was the traditional day of moving in those days.

2. At that time Lessebo forge was located in Hovmantorp parish. Parish boundaries have changed and it is now Lessebo parish.

3. Precautions to avoid a fire were paramount. Cooking was restricted to a small area by the foremast on the main deck. The fire was contained within a raised brick box, with a chimney to disperse sparks and smoke. They probably suppressed sparks even further by using charcoal rather than wood.

4. She was the wife of Bergsrådet Johan Lorentz Aschan. Bergsråd was the second highest title of Bergkollegium, the nationwide authority of mining and manufacture in Sweden. We will learn more about Bergsrådet in later chapters.

5. Today this area would be referred to as the south shore of South Center Lake. At that time Chisago Lake was just one large lake called Big Lake. The Swedes sometimes called it Swede Lake.

6. Glader Cemetery is situated on this hill at the shore of the little bay. Elin was the first burial in the cemetery.

About sister Christina's life at Husartorpet · · ·

1. After King Gustav Vasa broke his word and violated the truce of Christmas 1842, he brutally crushed the Småland Dacke rebellion. The Smålanders have never forgotten. Afterward the king created a special Småland Cavalry Regiment, later known as the Hussars. The

regiment was distributed about, with one or more soldiers assigned to a parish. The local farmers were to provide a small cottage [*torp*], about 24 feet long, and other facilities to maintain a small farm. During periods when no cavalry soldier was placed on the croft, the farmers instead paid a fee to the military and were allowed to take in tenants on the croft.

How Christina and her family sailed to North America · · ·

1. A "companion" was an unmarried noble woman of limited means, accompanying a woman of wealth. She acted as confidant, nurse, nanny or performed other tasks appropriate to her status.
2. Anders was later known as Andrew Taylor in America.
3. It was on the west shore of what is now South Center Lake just south of Lindstrom.
4. It is now known as South Lindstrom Lake.

How the party of Smålanders experienced living hell · · ·

1. The son was Carl Magnusson (Charles Magnuson in America) and the daughter Gustava (Magnusdotter) Strand.
2. Nordmansförbundet (*Norwegian Federation*) was a Norwegian magazine.
3. Grosse Isle is in the Isle-aux-Grues archipelago in the Gulf of St. Lawrence and means "Big Island" in French.
4. A custodian had taken care of the money until Gustav became of age, according to the law.

About emigrants from Älmeboda · · ·

1. Paupers were auctioned to the person who was willing to charge the least amout of money to support them. They were treated in a manner similar to foster care in America.
2. Pietism was an influential movement in Lutheranism that combined its emphasis on biblical doctrine with the Reformed emphasis on individual piety and living a vigorous Christian life.

155

How Samuel Pettersson found his mother's namesake · · ·

1. This refers to the hour between night and dawn, the hour when most people die; when sleep is deepest; when nightmares are most real; the hour when the sleepless are haunted by their deepest fears.
2. The Swedish text is as follows:
   > Håll käften på dig klockareskit
   > Vem fan har bett dig komma hit?
   > Vi har bott här i sockna i 50 år
   > Nog fasen vet vi hur psalmerna går.

   Apologies to Magnus Gustafsson for taking liberties with the translation.
3. Johannes Dillner (1775- 1862) was a priest in Östra Ryd parish, Uppland, and had received musical training and possessed a beautiful voice. Like Martin Luther he considered congregational singing an important part of the service and believed the people would gladly sing if they could read the music and learn the melodies.
4. Prosten (*provost*) was a title of honor for a priest
5. Matts Hansson's party arrived aboard the brig Ambrosius in New York, together with Magnus Jonasson's party. Both groups journeyed on to Illinois about the same time or perhaps together.
6. That works out to about 80% interest a year or $1600 yearly interest on his $2000 debt.

About life and death in the old country

1. He was responsible for supervising a large farm or estate.

About Jonas Peter Falk, whose grave · · ·

1. Reval is now known as Tallin, the Capital of Estonia.
2. Viborg and Svensksund were in Finland, a part of Sweden at that time.
3. A skeppspund (*ship's pound*), is an antiquated unit of weight.
4. A married woman in those days always covered her hair in public.
5. Samuel Carlsson Agrell married the widow of Magnus Petersson after Magnus died in the Civil War. Magnus was the Linn siblings' first cousin. Samuel adopted her three children and later they had a child of their own. They lived next door to Carl Linn.

How an early emigrant returned home with nothing but sand

1. In Swedish an apprentice carpenter is called a gesäll (*journeyman*) and is allowed to practice his trade on a provisional basis. This English "play on words" doesn't work in Swedish.
2. See the information box on page 12.
3. Carolina is the oldest daughter of Daniel Jonasson, Johan's brother

About Glader's life after Elin's death · · ·

1. She was the sister of Eric and Johan Magnusson who married the Linn sisters.
2. The book is titled *A History of the Swedish-Americans of Minnesota*.

About the rise and fall of a member of the parliament · · ·

1. A cold was the cause listed in the churchbook, but there was a worldwide flu epidemic in 1842–3 that may have been involved.

About everyday life · · ·

1. A two-story house was quite prestigious for Swedish settlers. Several affluent families owned such houses in Porter's home village Tävelsås.

Maps

Countries of Scandinavia

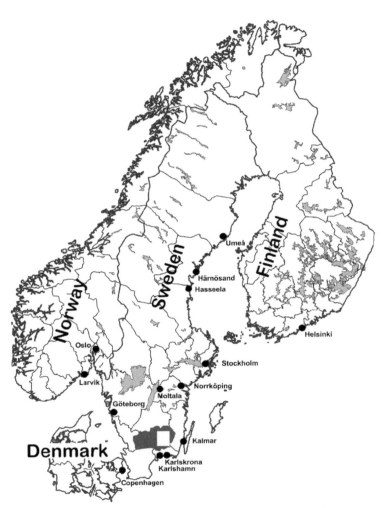

Four countries of Scandinavia were a significant source of immigrants to the United states in the late 1800s and early 1900s. The small square in Kronoberg county is enlarged on the facing page. Map: John Linn.

Kronoberg's emigration district

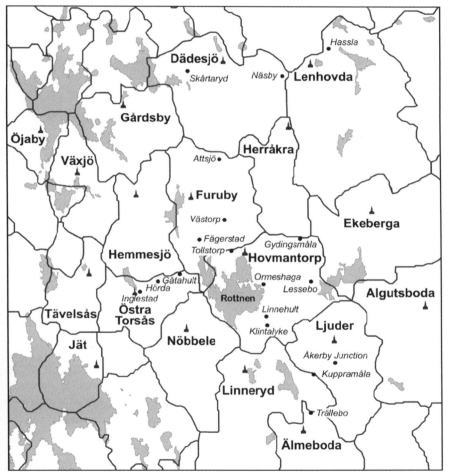

Many early immigrants to Chisago Lake came from a very small part of Sweden surounding Lake Rottnen in Kronoberg county, the small square on the facing page. Map: John Linn.

Index of Names

Index of Places

Bibliography

Arkiv Digital (AD) provided images for all original church books, general muster rolls and estate records.

About a poor Östgötlander who came to be a settler · · ·

[Bar88]   P. T. Barnum. *The life of P.T. Barnum*. 1888.

[Grö79]   Peter Grönberger. *Svenskarne i St. Croix-dalen, Minnesota*. (Svenska). 1879.

[Por12]   Robert B. Porter. *Emigrants at Worship: 125 years of Chisago Lake Methodism*. Lindstrom, Minnesota, 2012.

[Por83]   Robert B. Porter, ed. *Emigrants at Worship: 125 years of Chisago Lake Methodism*. Lindstrom, Minnesota, 1983.

[Rem07]   Jean Remes. *Discussion about Cajsa Lisa Pehrsdotter and Anders Svenson*. personal discussion. interview by Bodil Stefansson. Chisago County, Minnesota, 2007.

[Str10]   Algot E. Strand. *A History of the Swedish-Americans of Minnesota*. Lewis Publishing, 1910.

[Sve18]   Anders Svensson. *brev från Chisago Lake 5/1/1852*. Trans. by Bodil Stefansson. original letter in Swedish (1852). Svenska Emigrantinstitutet, 2018.

[Uno83]   Gustaf Unonius. *Minnen från en sjuttonårig vistelse i Nordvästra Amerika*. (Svenska). 1983.

[Upt08]   George P. Upton. *Musical Memories*. 1908.

How Magnus Jonasson emigrated from Linneryd · · ·

[Ado78]   Sven Adolfsson. "Bonde från Linneryd var Verklighetens Karl Oskar". (Svenska). I: *Kronobergsboken* (1978).

[Ado90]   Sven Adolfsson. "En bonde från Linneryd skrev första emigrantbrevet år 1852". (Svenska). I: *Tingsryds Allehanda* (1990).

[Bei00]   Ulf Beijbom. *Uppbrott från stenriket*. (Svenska). Emigrantinstitutets vänne, 2000.

[Hac90]   Lloyd C. Hackl. *The Wooden Shoe People*. Center City, MN: Minnesota Treasures, 1990.

[Hen70]   Axel Henriksson. "Den stora utvandringen". (Svenska). I: *Algutsboda sockenbok: del II* (1970).

[Joh73]   Emeroy Johnson. "Per Andersson's Letters from Chisago Lake." In: *Swedish-American Historical Quarterly* (1973).

[Lan77]	Gustav Lannerstock. *Vilhelm Moberg i Amerika.* (Svenska). 1977.

[Lin]   John Linn. "Linn Holmberg Family History." In: *personal database.*

[Lin05]   Olof Magny Linnell. *O.M. Linnell: His Life's Story.* reprint of 1917 book
           translated to English by Vernon Swenson. Amazon.com Kindle: John Linn,
           2005.

[Mat91]   Hans Mattson. *Reminiscences, Story of an Emigrant.* Saint Paul, Minnesota: D.
           D. Merrill Company, 1891.

[Tud11]   Mary Alice Tudor. *A New Life in a New Land.* Ed. by John Linn. reprint of
           unpublished manuscript (1967). Kindle online: Kenneth Tudor, John Linn,
           2011.

How Carl from Linnehult took the name Linn · · ·

[Afr]   "Afräkningsböcker (1830–1854)". (Svenska). I: vol. FIa:61. Lessebo
           bruksarkiv.

[Ber81]   Magnus Bergvall. *Resa i USA:s svenskbygd april 1981.* (Svenska). 1981.

[Car62]   Arvid Carlson. "Arvid Carlson inspelad gm Folke Hedblom 1962 Lindström,
           Minn". (Svenska). I: utg. av Folke Hedblom. Vol. USA 02 86A. Språk och
           folkminnesinstitutet, 1962.

[Kro33]   "Gårdar i Hovmantorp". (Svenska). I: *Släkt och Gårdsarkiv.*
           Kronobergsarkivet, 1833–1921, s. 38–348.

[Lin]   John Linn. "Linn Holmberg Family History." In: *personal database.*

[Lin99]   "Linnehult". (Svenska). I: *Fastighetshandlingar.* Vol. FIa:2. Lessebo
           bruksarkiv, 1899.

[Tud11]   Mary Alice Tudor. *A New Life in a New Land.* Ed. by John Linn. reprint of
           unpublished manuscript (1967). Kindle online: Kenneth Tudor, John Linn,
           2011.

How Glader emigrated with family and followers · · ·

[Ado68]   Sven Adolfsson. *Intervju med Oskar Johansson om Glader.* (Svenska). Växjö,
           Småland, Sweden: Svenska Emigrantinstitutet, 1968.

[Arv47]   Yngve Arvidsson, utg. *Hovmantorps kyrka Minnesskrift.* (Svenska). 1947.

[Berg53]   "Berget under Västorps Lambritsgård (1853)". (Svenska). I: *Säljbrev.*
           Vol. Konga härads dombok: AIa:157. Vadstena landsarkiv.

[Ble41]   Theodore Blegen. *The American Transition.* 1941.

[Blo06]   Milan Bloom. *Stories of the Chisago City Porter and Glader familys.* 2006.

[Chisp]   "Konstituerandet av och tidiga protokoll från Chisago Lake församlingen
           (1854–1968)". (Svenska). I: *Chisago Lake Lutheran Church archives.*
           Minnesota Historical Society.

| [Fra] | "Franklin King (1853-07-26)." In: *Passenger Lists of Vessels Arriving at New York, New York 1820–1897*. National Archives and Records Administration. |

[Gåra]   Hans Gårdman. *Hans Gårdman om Franklin King (1853)*. (Svenska). URL: www.jamestownswedes.org/p/1853%5C_29.

[Gårb]   Hans Gårdman. *Skeppslista för Franklin King aug. 1853 (1853)*. (Svenska). URL: www.jamestownswedes.org/p/ships-list.html.

[Hac90]   Lloyd C. Hackl. *The Wooden Shoe People*. Center City, MN: Minnesota Treasures, 1990.

[Hal]   Augustus F. Halgren. "Varning till emigranter (1854)". (Svenska). I: *tidningen Folkets Röst i Kalmar*. this site is no longer active. Kungliga biblioteket. URL: magasin.kb.se.

[Joh03]   Emeroy Johnson. "The first 100 years 1854–1954." In: *150 Years of Ministry. Chisago Lake Evangelical Lutheran Church 1854/2004*. Ed. by Carolyn F. Lystig. Minneapolis, Minnesota: Kirk House Publishers, 2003.

[Jon]   John Everett Jones. *The voyage of the sailing ship Franklin King in the summer of 1853*. URL: www.jamestownswedes.org/p/ships-list.html.

[Mob]   Vilhelm Moberg. (Svenska). I: *Foton från forskningsarbetet för utvandrarromanen i Amerika*. Vol. 18:1. Svenska Emigrantinstitutet.

[Nor84]   Eric Norelius. *The pioneer Swedish settlements and Swedish Lutheran Churches in America 1845–1860*. Rock Island, Illinois: Augustana Historical Society, 1984.

[Soc00]   *Näringsproblem i vård och omsorg: prevention och behandling*. (Svenska). 2000.

[Sol]   Børge Solem. *Sailing ship provision*. the web site is nolonger active. URL: www.norwayheritage.com (visited on 2015).

[Trib53] "Ships arrival in New York (1853-07-26)." In: *New York Daily Tribune* (07/26/1853).

About sister Christina's life at Husartorpet · · ·

[Afr]   "Afräkningsböcker (1830–1854)". (Svenska). I: vol. FIa:61. Lessebo bruksarkiv.

[Höj95]   Pia Höjeberg. *Helena Malhiems Barnmorskelära 1756*. (Svenska). 1995.

[Hus38]   *Torpsyn på Husartorpet i Västorp*. (Svenska). Lessebo bruksarkiv, 1838.

[Nil47]   Johan Nilsson. "Om havandeskap, födsel, dop, kyrktagning, lyten, m.m. i Allbo under gångna tider". (Svenska). I: *Värendsbygder* (1947).

[Tru99]   "Truvedsgård". (Svenska). I: *Fastighetshandlingar*. Vol. FIa:61. Lessebo bruksarkiv, 1899.

[Vad30]   "Uppgifter om barnmorskor inkomna med anledning av domkapitlets cirkulär". (Svenska). I: F VII:19 (1830).

How Christina and her family sailed to North America · · ·

[Cam54]   "Ship Cambria." In: *Passenger and Crew Lists 1820–1963 (New York)*. National
            Archives and Records Administration.

[Car11]   Ben Carlson. *The Family History of Andreas and Ingrid Maria Carlson/Taylor.*
            2011.

[Lin05]   Olof Magny Linnell. *O.M. Linnell: His Life's Story.* reprint of 1917 book
            translated to English by Vernon Swenson. Amazon.com Kindle: John Linn,
            2005.

[Nel]   John Carl Nelson. *Nils Daniel Andersson 1807–1869.* URL:
            www.jsenterprises.com/john/famhist/html/I44.html
            (visited on 2019).

[Str10]   Algot E. Strand. *A History of the Swedish-Americans of Minnesota.* Lewis
            Publishing, 1910.

How the party of Smålanders experienced living hell · · ·

[Alm74]   Sten Almqvist. "Amerikapionjärerna". (Svenska). I: *Öjaby Hembygds och
            kulturförening* (1974).

[Blo06]   Milan Bloom. *Stories of the Chisago City Porter and Glader familys.* 2006.

[Jen08]   Cock Jenssen H. "Emigrantfart for 50-60 aar siden". (Norsk). I:
            Nordmansförbundet I (1908).

[JJJ08]   John A. Johnson, Alice E. Johnson, and Laura A. Johnson. *Hon J.A. Johnson:
            A partial copy of his letters, travels and addresses.* 1908.

[Lea08]   Earl W. Leaf. *Chisago County Pioneers: Biographical Sketches of Early Settlers.*
            2008.

[Lea10]   Earl W. Leaf. *Carl Gustaf Chellberg och Lovisa Charlotta.* e-mail. 05/2010.

[Lin]   John Linn. "Linn Holmberg Family History." In: *personal database*.

[Lun71]   Georg Lundgren. "Emigranter från Östra Thorsås samt Hemmessjö-Tegnaby
            socknar". (Svenska). I: *Östra Hembygdsförenings årsbok nr 12* (1971).

[Mor06]   Wayne Morrison. *Family Stories.* e-mail to John Linn. 2006.

[Ohl71]   Carl Ohlin. "En Amerikaresa 1854". (Svenska). I: *Östra Thorsås
            Hembygdsförenings årsbok* (1971).

[Smp01]   "Östra Thorsåsbo borgmästare i Amerika". (Svenska). I: *Smålands-Posten*
            (1901-12-09).

[Str10]   Algot E. Strand. *A History of the Swedish-Americans of Minnesota.* Lewis
            Publishing, 1910.

About emigrants from Älmeboda · · ·

[Blo06] Milan Bloom. *The Bloom/Collin Family History.* 2006.

[Col] Gustaf Colllin. *Gustav Collins självbiografi.* (Svenska).

[Hac90] Lloyd C. Hackl. *The Wooden Shoe People.* Center City, MN: Minnesota Treasures, 1990.

[Lag62] Ebba Lagergren. "Fäderna berätta". (Svenska). I: *Älmebodaboken* (1962).

[Nil36] "Rättegång angående underhåll till Samuel Nilssons syster med familj". (Svenska). I: vol. Konga härads dombok: AIa:105. Vadstena landsarkiv, 1836.

[Por83] Robert B. Porter, ed. *Emigrants at Worship: 125 years of Chisago Lake Methodism.* Lindstrom, Minnesota, 1983.

[Ros11] Anton Rose. *Gustaf Collin and Gustaf Bloom.* (Svenska). Med redigering och tillägg av Milan Bloom. 2011.

[Wen71] Gunnel Wendel. *Åkianismen och Utvandrarromanen.* (Svenska). 1971.

[Wood54] "Ship Woodbury." In: *Passenger and Crew Lists 1820–1963 (Massachusetts).* National Archives and Records Administration.

How Samuel Pettersson found his mother's namesake · · ·

[Car15] August Carlsson. "August Carlsson om prosten Andersson och lekstugor". (Svenska). I: *Acc nr 869, No 71* (1915).

[Chis54] "Förteckningen av de första medlemmarna i Chisago Lake Lutheran Church". (Svenska). I: *Chisago Lake Lutheran Church archives.* Center city, Minnesota, 1854.

[Chisp] "Konstituerandet av och tidiga protokoll från Chisago Lake församlingen (1854–1968)". (Svenska). I: *Chisago Lake Lutheran Church archives.* Minnesota Historical Society.

[GG86] Magnus Gustafsson och Björn Gidstam. *Visor i Småland.* (Svenska). 1986.

[HPF01] Lloyd Hackl, Robert Porter, and Leilani Freeman. *A History of Chisago County 1851–2001.* 2001.

[Joh03] Emeroy Johnson. "The first 100 years 1854–1954." In: *150 Years of Ministry. Chisago Lake Evangelical Lutheran Church 1854/2004.* Ed. by Carolyn F. Lystig. Minneapolis, Minnesota: Kirk House Publishers, 2003.

[Lan65] "Chisago Lake Township Pioneer Land Owners." In: *Chisago County Historical Society archives* (1865).

[Mat91] Hans Mattson. *Reminiscences, Story of an Emigrant.* Saint Paul, Minnesota: D. D. Merrill Company, 1891.

[Nor55] Eric Norelius. "Brev från Norelius". (Svenska). I: *Hemlandet.* Galesburg, Illinois: Svenska Emigrantinstitutet, 1855-12-01.

[Nor84] Eric Norelius. *The pioneer Swedish settlements and Swedish Lutheran Churches in America 1845–1860.* Rock Island, Illinois: Augustana Historical Society, 1984.

[Oli73]   Karl Olin. *Chisago Lake församlingen i Minnesota. Förteckning över de äldsta medlemmarna 1855–1867.* (Svenska). 1973.

About life and death in the old country

[And35]   Gerward Andersson. " Wilhelm Johansson om begravningar i Västorp". (Svenska). I: *Acc nr 4589* (1935).

[And56]   "Nils Andersson". (Svenska). I: *Bouppteckning.* Vol. Konga härads dombok: FII:40. 1856, s. 937.

[Bei96]   Ulf Beijbom. *Amerikaminnen. Berättelser i utvandrarbygd.* (Svenska). Norstedt, 1996.

[Håk56]   "Nils Håkanssons". (Svenska). I: *Bouppteckning.* Vol. Konga härads dombok: FII:40. 1856, s. 1103.

[Kro33]   "Gårdar i Hovmantorp". (Svenska). I: *Släkt och Gårdsarkiv.* Kronobergsarkivet, 1833–1921, s. 38–348.

[Lan90]   Maria Landin. *Gårdarna i Västorp.* (Svenska). www.hembygd.se/hovmantorp-furuby/gardarna-i-vastorp, 1990.

[Sto72]   Jonas Stolt. *Byskomakaren Jonas Stolts minnen.* (Svenska). 1972.

[Tud11]   Mary Alice Tudor. *A New Life in a New Land.* Ed. by John Linn. reprint of unpublished manuscript (1967). Kindle online: Kenneth Tudor, John Linn, 2011.

About Jonas Peter Falk, whose grave · · ·

[Afr]   "Afräkningsböcker (1817–1840)". (Svenska). I: Lessebo bruksarkiv.

[And48]   "Anna Maria Andersdotter". (Svenska). I: *Bouppteckning.* Vol. Konga härads dombok: FII:36. 1848, s. 1069.

[Eks27]   Johan Ekstrand. "Metereologiske observationer hållne i Vexiö år 1827". (Svenska). I: *Vetenskapsakademien* SE/RA/420468/1/18 (1827).

[Gyd30]   "Gydingsmåla". (Svenska). I: *Fastighetshandlingar 1757–1905.* Vol. FIa:52. Lessebo bruksarkiv, 1830–1854.

[Hog]   Hans Hogman. *Kalmar regemente.* (Svenska). URL: http://www.hhogman.se/regiments_infantry-4.htm#x1_Kalmar-regemente_I20.

[Joh60]   "Gustaf Johansson". (Svenska). I: *Bouppteckning.* Vol. Konga härads dombok: FII:18. 1860, s. 1559.

[Kal]   "Andra Majorens Compani No 70". (Svenska). I: *Kalmar Regemente Generalmönsterrullor,* s. 415–419.

[Lin]   John Linn. "Linn Holmberg Family History." In: *personal database.*

[LR00]   Lars-Olof Larsson och Leif Rubensson. *Från blästerbruk till bruksdöd.* (Svenska). 2000.

[Mob50]   Villhelm Moberg. *Den okända släkten*. (Svenska). 1950.

[Pro55]   "Sockenstämmoprotokoll 1855 - 1862". (Svenska). I: *Vadstena landsarkiv.*
             Vol. KIa:4. Hovmantorps kyrkoarkiv.

[Str60]   "Anna Lena Carlsdotter Streling". (Svenska). I: *Bouppteckning*. Vol. Konga
             härads dombok: FII:42. 1860, s. 757.

[Ten69]   Enar Tenggren. "Julatorpet – änkan Falk och hennes fem pojkar". (Svenska).
             I: *Hovmantorp-Furuby Årskrönika* (1969).

How an early emigrant returned home with nothing but sand

[Ado78]   Sven Adolfsson. "Bonde från Linneryd var Verklighetens Karl Oskar".
             (Svenska). I: *Kronobergsboken* (1978).

[Lin05]   Olof Magny Linnell. *O.M. Linnell: His Life's Story*. reprint of 1917 book
             translated to English by Vernon Swenson. Amazon.com Kindle: John Linn,
             2005.

[Tud11]   Mary Alice Tudor. *A New Life in a New Land*. Ed. by John Linn. reprint of
             unpublished manuscript (1967). Kindle online: Kenneth Tudor, John Linn,
             2011.

About Glader's life after Elin's death · · ·

[Ado69]   Sven Adolfsson. *Emigrant från Hjortsberga som blev präst i Amerika.*
             (Svenska). Svenska Emigrantinstitutet, 1969.

[Chisp]   "Konstituerandet av och tidiga protokoll från Chisago Lake församlingen
             (1854–1968)". (Svenska). I: *Chisago Lake Lutheran Church archives.*
             Minnesota Historical Society.

[Fau06]   Gidget Faubion. "Om familjen Glader". (Svenska). I: *E-post* (2006–2007).

[Joh03]   Emeroy Johnson. "The first 100 years 1854–1954." In: *150 Years of Ministry.*
             Chisago Lake Evangelical Lutheran Church 1854/2004. Ed. by
             Carolyn F. Lystig. Minneapolis, Minnesota: Kirk House Publishers, 2003.

[Lin05]   Olof Magny Linnell. *O.M. Linnell: His Life's Story*. reprint of 1917 book
             translated to English by Vernon Swenson. Amazon.com Kindle: John Linn,
             2005.

[Nor84]   Eric Norelius. *The pioneer Swedish settlements and Swedish Lutheran
             Churches in America 1845–1860*. Rock Island, Illinois: Augustana Historical
             Society, 1984.

[Por07]   Robert B Porter. *The Methodist Church of Ki-Chi-Saga*. 2007.

[Por89]   Robert B Porter. *The Secrets of Glader: Minnesota's Oldest Swedish Cemetery.*
             1989.

[Str10]   Algot E. Strand. *A History of the Swedish-Americans of Minnesota*. Lewis
             Publishing, 1910.

About the rise and fall of a member of the parliament · · ·

[Afr17]   "Afräkningsböcker". (Svenska). I: vol. GIa. Lessebo bruksarkiv.

[And52]   "Uppteckning Anders Ruth". (Svenska). I: *August Andersson berättar.*
               Vol. *063158. Lunds universitets kyrkoarkiv, 1952.

[And56]   "Martha Andersdotter". (Svenska). I: *Bouppteckning.* Vol. Konga härads
               dombok: FII:40. 1856, s. 1119.

[Car62]   Arvid Carlson. "Arvid Carlson inspelad gm Folke Hedblom 1962 Lindström,
               Minn". (Svenska). I: utg. av Folke Hedblom. Vol. USA 02 86A. Språk och
               folkminnesinstitutet, 1962.

[Lin08]   Marie Lindstedt Cronberg. *Heder och ära i tidigmodern tid.* (Svenska). 2008.

[Maga37]   "Magnus Jonssons inteckning". (Svenska). I: vol. AIa:107. Konga härads
               dombok, 1837.

[Magb36]   "Rättegång mot Magnus Jonsson". (Svenska). I: vol. AIa:104. Vadstena
               landsarkiv, 1836.

[Magc36]   "Ormeshagahult. Fastighetshandlingar 1806–1905". (Svenska). I: vol. FIa:63.
               Lessebo bruksarkiv, 1836.

[Nei81]   Edward D Neill. "Explorers and Pioneers of Minnesota." In: *History of
               Washington County and the St. Croix Valley.* Ed. by George E. Warner and
               Charles M. Foote. Minneapolis, Minnesota: North Star Publishing Company,
               1881.

[Tra46]   Merle Travis. *Sixteen Tons.* Broadcast Music, Inc. (BMI), 1946.

About everyday life · · ·

[Por32]   Frank Porter. "Porter Family Rememberances." In: *unpublished manuscript.*
               later published in Hackl, *The Wooden-Shoe People* (1986). 1932.

About John Linn

I became involved with family history long after both my parents were gone. "Why didn't I ask them before they died?" was my constant lament. Genealogy in those days was mostly digging through musty documents in libraries and scrutinizing old microfilm records ordered from the LDS archives. As I began gathering my parent's memories in photographs, I realized that most were not annotated in any way—"I recognize my grandpa, but who is **that** old guy?"

The research to find the answers consumed a lot of time and effort, even though I had a family in need of attention, a house that required a lot of improvement, several aging vehicles with questionable reliability and too many hobbies. I also had this nagging problem of a real job that always got in the way.

My grandfather did leave me one legacy—a tattered and unpublished book titled *A Good Life in a Good Land* written by his older sister Alice (Linn) Tudor about her life growing up in Lindstrom on the shore of Linn Lake. She recounted the story of her subsequent move west to the tiny town of Sumas on the Canadian border in Washington State, the place where I was born and raised. She noted how coincidentally similar her parent's and grandparent's immigration story was to Vilhelm Moberg's *The Emigrants* novels. I had to read all four volumes of his books.

I always had an interest in graphics arts (too many hobbies) and decided to publish an annotated version of her memoirs so it would be more accessible to the rest of the family. Genealogy became more seductive when the actual stories behind the faded records revealed themselves.

I also was enticed by another book, *The Secrets of Glader* by Robert Porter. At that time I had discovered enough family history to recognize that several of those long dead Swedes buried in Glader Cemetery were related to me and I suspected most had been connected to each other in Sweden before coming to Chisago Lake. Having just learned how to read musty electronic church microfilm records downloaded from Gedline, I delved in and confirmed it. (How electrons become musty, I will never know.) It proved to be a challenge reading Swedish documents written in a language I don't speak; in an archaic handwritten dialect with old and erratic spelling; containing smudges, ink blots,

179

poor image quality and missing pages; with mistakes of fact and sometimes outright lies; employing names seemingly changing at random; and of course often sneaking in text in Latin. I have since learned that modern-day Swedes have difficulty reading this stuff too. But these records are just boring facts. I was more interested in the drama and intrigue behind them.

I began contacting people in Sweden who might know more, and eventually met a nice Swedish lady named Bodil Stefansson who was writing a book titled *En man som hetade Glader* about her husband's family. We discovered Ingvar was part of my family, too. About that time, I retired from my job of 33 years as a research computer scientist, engineer and technical manager in the semiconductor industry. My wife and I had time to travel and we took a cruise around the Baltic, including a visit with Bodil and Ingvar in Småland.

She was writing true stories about people recorded in the ancient records that she and Ingvar had learned to read and interpret. We got a tour of the many historical things and places related to my family. Sweden seemed eerily familiar and the visit was a goldmine for Swedish emigrant history. We hit it off and have been working together periodically ever since. I have learned so much.

I have published several books about family history. The latest is a memoir my wife Ginny wrote titled *The Other Side of Crazy: My Odyssey to Insanity and Back*. It is a story of hope, recovery and redemption for those suffering from severe mental illness.

And I still have too many hobbies, but life is good.

John Linn

Printed in Great Britain
by Amazon

57946257R00111